Mediterranean

HOT

Mediterranean

Spicy Dishes from Southern Italy, Greece, Turkey & North Africa

HOT

AGLAIA KREMEZI

Illustrations by Linda Frichtel

ARTISAN New York

To Sarah-Jane Freymann, my intellectual coach

Editor: Ann ffolliott
Production director: Hope Koturo

Published in 1996 by Artisan,
a division of Workman Publishing Company, Inc.
708 Broadway
New York, NY 10003-9555

Library of Congress Cataloging-in-Publication Data

Kremezi, Aglaia.
    Mediterranean Hot : spicy dishes from southern Italy, Greece, Turkey,
and North Africa / by Aglaia Kremezi : illustrations by Linda Frichtel.
    Includes bibliographical references and index.
    ISBN 1-885183-26-7
    1. Cookery, Mediterranean. 2. Cookery (Hot Peppers) I. Title.
TX725.M35K74 1996
641.59182'2—dc20   95-46569

Printed in Italy
10 9 8 7 6 5 4 3 2 1
First Printing

Contents

Introduction

This book is the result of my love affair with hot, vigorous, zesty Mediterranean food—dishes bursting with color, flavor, and aroma, based on the seasonal produce of this sunny corner of the world. Chilies are not usually associated with Mediterranean cooking, but they have a long history here. The Mediterranean use of chilies is more subtle than that of Mexico, India, and Asia. The spiciest Mediterranean recipes, which are found in Tunisia and Algeria, are never as blisteringly hot as some familiar "hot" dishes. You can enjoy these recipes even if you don't consider yourself a chili aficionado.

This book contains recipes that I have collected from around the Mediterranean for delicious salads, spreads, sauces, soups, one-pot dishes, and desserts that are easy to prepare with readily available ingredients. These are the dishes I serve to my family and friends. I have included recipes traditionally prepared with lots of chilies and other pungent spices, but also some classic Mediterranean dishes that are greatly improved when more spices are added. All of these dishes are based on the traditional, healthy Mediterranean diet of grains, dried beans, vegetables, olive oil, fish, and just a little bit of meat and dairy products (usually in the form of cheese or yogurt).

Spicy foods were part of my teenage rebellion. Strong *skordalia* (garlic sauce) was the most highly flavored food served in our house. When I discovered mustard I started adding masses of it to everything, much to my father's dismay. Once I tasted traditional, highly spiced Greek foods, I couldn't believe that the Greeks had been satisfied with bland dishes for so long. Spices are like that; once you taste them, you can't forget them. From then on, everything tastes insipid without their piquancy and aroma.

Spices in the Mediterranean

Greece, caught between West and East, demonstrates a split personality in its use of spices. Those who consider themselves European avoid using most spices, especially cumin, which they associate with the years Greece spent under Ottoman rule. On the other hand, some traditionalists continue to cook with spices as their ancestors did.

Greece is not the only Mediterranean country that holds contradictory feelings about spices. The European part of the Mediterranean has almost forgotten the fragrant, spicy foods of its past, while the countries on the African and Middle Eastern shores are a kind of gastronomic time capsule whose inhabitants still eat foods similar to those consumed there in ancient and medieval times.

Spices never went out of fashion in North Africa and the Middle East, as they did in Europe. As Fernand Braudel writes in his classic *The*

Mediterranean and the Mediterranean World at the time of Philip II, "In the sixteenth century, a native of the Mediterranean, whenever he might come from, would never feel out of place in any part of the sea. To later colonial settlers their journey simply meant finding in a new place the same trees and plants, the same food on the table that they had known in their homeland." While the food eaten in Spain, France, and Italy has changed dramatically since the sixteenth century, in Tunisia, Algeria, and Morocco, one can still find dishes consumed on a regular basis that are described in ancient papyruses. Combinations of spices, nuts, and sweet and sour flavors that were common in Europe during the Middle Ages are still used in the traditional dishes of most Arab countries. These dishes may give us a realistic idea about the flavors of European food served before the Renaissance.

Visitors today are amazed at the important role spices play in the souk, the picturesque open markets of North Africa. Sacks full of dark red or brick-colored sweet and hot paprika, bright yellow turmeric powder, fragrant cinnamon, cardamom, cumin and cloves, saffron threads (or its cheaper substitute, marigold petals) and other seeds, dried roots, nuts, and barks are displayed with flair. The quantities startle unsuspecting European and American tourists who are used to purchasing spices in tiny jars in the supermarket. I have overheard them wondering if the spices are displayed this way to give them colorful photo opportunities. This couldn't be farther from the truth. If you spend some time near a North African spice shop, you will observe the local people buying cumin,

caraway seeds, paprika, and peppercorns in paper bags, by weight, much as we buy coffee beans.

Because immigrants from all around the Mediterranean have brought their hot sauces and relishes to Israel, it offers a particularly rich culinary experience. Visitors can find an astonishing array of chili-flavored condiments at the ubiquitous kebab and falafel stands. The émigrés from Ethiopia and Yemen have brought the spicy flavors of those two countries to the Mediterranean palate. When I traveled to Israel, I was fascinated to see how some hot condiments, such as the fiery *zhug* and the intriguing *hilbeh* sauce, have already become Mediterranean classics.

The Spices of Paradise

The heat and aroma of exotic seeds, barks, nuts, and oils invite us to places where the sun shines brightly all year long. Many spices originated in the "mysterious" East, an almost mythical region to many Europeans. The ruling classes paid fortunes to bring a tiny piece of this marvelous place to their damp and cold castles. "No medieval writer could envision Paradise without the smell or taste of spices. Whether the poetically described gardens served saints or lovers, the atmosphere was inevitably infused with the rare intoxicating fragrance of cinnamon, nutmeg, ginger, and cloves," writes Bridget Ann Henisch in her book *Feast and Fast.* Spices were purchased at any price to enliven dull and monotonous foods.

Many Northern Europeans and Americans of Northern European descent still think that civilized individuals eat bland foods while spicy foods are for less-developed countries. But this is changing; spicy foods are now sought after by today's cooks in both America and Europe, many of whom grew up eating unseasoned foods. And although the fabled East of our forebears has been de-mystified, modern research has shown us that there is more to spices than heat, taste, and aroma.

The widespread belief that in previous centuries exotic flavorings were used primarily to mask the taste of spoiled foods is simplistic. It is true that some spices were used for their preserving properties, but this alone would hardly make a seed or a piece of bark so precious that people would risk their lives traveling to the ends of the earth for it. Spices would never have become status symbols or have been offered as tokens of love and friendship if they were used merely to cover the taste of rotten meat.

To understand the importance of spices fully, we must go back in time to the first civilizations that flourished around the Mediterranean. Pepper, cinnamon, and other fragrant flavorings arrived in Europe and the Middle East long before the Middle Ages. They were imported to Egypt, Greece, and Rome even before classical times. Peppercorns were found in the mummy of Ramses II (second century B.C.), because pepper was used in the mummification process. There are extant recipes for therapeutic drinks and ointments that include black and white pepper. Hippocrates, the great Greek doctor who lived from 460–377, B.C., used ground peppercorns mixed with wine or vinegar in some of his prescriptions.

Ancient Greeks burned aromatic herbs and spices before and with the meat that was offered to the gods as sacrifices. A passage from the Bible mentions cinnamon and myrrh used for this purpose. We know that the sacrificial meats were eaten by the priests, so it is safe to conclude that they were among the first Europeans to savor spice-flavored food.

If we believe the many references to food that have survived in Athenaeus' *Deipnosophistae*, (a compilation of fragments of earlier Greek writings) classical dishes were very highly spiced. Here is a description of a kind of meatball called a *myma*—an ancestor to the Middle Eastern *kofta*—taken from the writings of Artemidorus, a disciple of Aristophanes of the fifth century, B.C.:

> *A myma of any kind of meat, including fowl, should be made by cutting up the tender parts of the meat into small pieces, mashing in the viscera, intestine, and blood, and spicing with vinegar, toasted cheese, silphium, cumin, fresh and dried thyme, savory, fresh and dried coriander, horn onion, roasted common peeled onion, or poppy-head raisins or honey or the seeds of an acid pomegranate.*

Silphium was a much-loved ancient herb with a strong, garlicky taste. It is similar to asafoetida, which is still a common ingredient of Indian curries. Silphium is no longer used in the Mediterranean, but the rest of the herbs and spices mentioned by Artemidorus could easily be part of a modern Middle Eastern or North African dish.

According to ancient theories of medicine, herbs and spices added to basic foods were used not only to improve flavor but also to provide the body with healing substances. Some were believed to enhance sexual potency in men, while others were taken by women either to aid them in becoming pregnant or to prevent pregnancies. Many of these ancient theories have been shown to be effective by modern research. Silphium, for example, contains substances that act as a female contraceptive. The concept of illness-preventing foods has made a strong comeback today.

To this day, many of the classic spice mixtures of North Africa and the Middle East contain elements that have nothing to do with flavor or aroma, and are added only for "Adam's health," as an Ethiopian spice merchant told me, referring to a mysterious grain that he insisted was part of the classic Berbere mixture. Moroccan *Ras el Hanout*, the most aromatic of all spice mixtures, contains the microscopic bright green insects called cantharides (the notorious Spanish Fly).

If we consume quantities of pepper, ginger, and the chilies that were brought to Europe after its discovery of the New World, we experience a burning sensation, Heat and fire are directly associated with love and passion, so it is not strange that all hot spices were considered aphrodisiacs by Romans and Aztecs alike, while monks in some medieval monasteries banned chilies and hot spices from the diets of religious and chaste men. A Spanish folk proverb suggests that God created sweet peppers and the Devil twisted them to create the hot ones. Interestingly enough, modern research has shown that the burning, almost painful sensation inflicted by the capsaicin in pepper and chilies stimulates the brain to produce endorphins—natural painkillers—which create a euphoric sensation, like that of a runner's high.

In view of all this, it is not so hard to understand why countless wars and expeditions—causing many deaths—were launched in order to secure the supply of spices to Europe, and, in the process, changing the map and altering the landscape of distant countries.

We can understand how the taste of pepper—by far the most popular of all spices—and other exotic condiments must have improved the flavor of everyday food. In ancient and medieval times, although the rich could afford to eat more meat than the poor, their daily diet was based on grain porridge and a few seasonal vegetables and greens, which would have become extremely boring without the zest provided by pepper and other condiments.

Exotic flavorings and aromatics were not just used to make food taste good but were also status symbols, frequently accorded the same respect as gold and silver. Peppercorns were sometimes used as currency and were even given as ransom. Alaric, the fourth-century king, demanded 3,000 pounds of pepper from the defeated Romans in addition to gold and silver. Byzantine emperors sent spices to appease foreign rulers. We know that Theodosius III sent a "large bale" of pepper to the Attila the Hun.

The Travels of the Chili Pepper

The introduction of chilies played an important part in the disappearance of the spicy high-status dishes of the Renaissance and Baroque eras, suggests anthropologist Sophie Coe in *America's First Cuisines*. Chilies were cheap; they needn't be imported, increasing in price as they passed from one middleman to the next. Chilies could be cultivated locally around the Mediterranean, and even the poor could feast on their fiery taste.

As spices lost their status, they consequently fell out of fashion. Newly imported foodstuffs such as coffee, tea, chocolate, vanilla, and sugar became the culinary status symbols of the seventeenth century, much as spices had been up until the end of the sixteenth century, suggests Wolfgang Schivelbuch in his *Tastes of Paradise*. He notes that the French led the way to moderately spiced dishes, and the rest of Europe followed, putting western cuisine on the path to what it is today.

On the other hand, common people now had the chance to experience the invigorating taste of chilies. The shift of the taste for spicy foods from the upper to the lower classes must have contributed to the division of the world into those who ate and those who avoided chilies, making the matter a moral issue in the nineteenth century, as Sophie Coe has noted. She mentions that the French general Lafayette considered chilies to be not only bad for the health, but also bad morally. Coe also quotes a letter written in 1668 by John Evelyn, ambassador extraordinary to the court of Spain, who compares the lovely peppers growing on his pepper plant to polished coral. But he suggests that if you ate even the smallest piece you would set your throat on fire, which could cause death.

The chilies of the Americas were first cultivated in the old world not in Portugal or Spain, but on the west coast of Africa, where the Portuguese ships stopped on their way back from the New World. From West Africa chilies were taken to the western coast of India, then to the Portuguese colony of Macao, and from there to Philippines, Japan, and the Spice Islands. The inhabitants of all these places found chilies to be an ideal inexpensive seasoning. It is believed that chilies returned to America with the slaves brought from Africa on English and Dutch ships.

When chilies finally began to be used as a condiment in Europe—about 50 years after they were first brought from the New World—they were associated with India, the place where most spices came from. According to food historian Louis Szathmary, author of a detailed account of the wanderings of the chili around Europe entitled "Paprika: The Gift of Columbus to the Hungarian Kitchen" (presented at the 1992 Oxford Symposium on Food), when the Ottomans invaded India

in the fifteenth century, they immediately under-
stood the value of the chili and brought it back
to Europe, distributing it throughout their vast
empire, which included North Africa, the Middle
East, and the Balkans. As Szathmary points out,
the Ottomans brought their families and slaves
with them to the countries they occupied. They
didn't import foodstuffs from their homelands, but
relied on local agriculture. The Turks liked chilies,
and they spread the cultivation of "Turkish pepper"
to Hungary, Bulgaria, Serbia, and northern Greece.
Chili cultivation produced the famous paprika, the
most important agricultural product of Hungary to
this day. Near the city of Aridea in northern
Greece, chilies were cultivated extensively from the
sixteenth century. Old records show that the region
was protected by special laws because its peppers
were much appreciated by the Turkish Sultans.

Sweet or Hot?

In some European countries people prefer sweet
peppers. Jean Andrews, in the introduction to her
book *Red Hot Peppers*, writes about the difference
in the use of peppers around the Mediterranean.
The sweeter capsicums were favored in Spain and
Italy, while the Ottomans distributed hotter peppers and spices—"more Indian in nature"—in the
Balkans and the Eastern Mediterranean.

In America there is a clear distinction
between different kinds of chilies and their partic-
ular flavors, but around the Mediterranean—and
throughout Europe—chilies are only distinguished
by their level of heat. The Italians call the hot
chilies used mostly in the cooking of Sicily and
Calabria by the generic name *peperoncini* (small

peppers), while the chili powder produced in the
northern Greece is simply called *kokino piperi*
(red pepper).

The chilies cultivated around the Mediterranean since the fifteenth century have produced
many local varieties, suited to the soil and the cli-
matic conditions of each country. In Greece
alone—according to Stelios Samaras, of the Greek
National Bank of Agricultural Seeds—there are
some forty different varieties of hot peppers, varying in shape, size, and degree of heat. In Turkey
and Syria there are delicious moderately hot peppers that are dried and crushed to produce Near
East or Aleppo pepper, much appreciated for its
rich taste.

It is difficult to suggest exact substitutes for
Mediterranean peppers among the different American chilies. The sun and the mostly dry climate
of the Mediterranean makes for very tasty hot
and sweet peppers. But ironically, most of the
peppers that reach the European supermarkets and
the big restaurant kitchens today come not from
the Mediterranean, but from Dutch greenhouses.
These gorgeous looking but sun-deprived and
tasteless vegetables are sold throughout the European part of the Mediterranean. Even the hot
chilies available in local farmer's markets are tend-
ing to become more and more uniform and less
and less flavorful, as a result of new varieties
developed for growing in greenhouses. Let's hope
that independent growers with a passion for flavor
will start to experiment with the many traditional
hot peppers of the Mediterranean, now that spicy
food is becoming increasingly popular in Europe,
America, and the rest of the world.

Acknowledgments

I owe more than I can express to Artisan publisher Leslie Stoker, for her enthusiasm and support. Ann ffolliott, my editor and friend, once more helped me to organize this book—never an easy task—and I am ever so grateful. I would also like to thank Jim Wageman, Jennifer Hong, Russell Hassell, Hope Koturo, Beth Wareham, Eliza Kunkel, Carole Berglie, Marcia Pomerantz, Cathy Dorsey, and Linda Frichtel.

This book is the product of extensive research on location in many of the countries that surround the Mediterranean, and it could not have been completed without the help of the region's friendly and generous inhabitants. I extend my thanks to all of them.

Among them, I would first like to thank the people who helped me in Israel: Dalia Carmel in New York put me in touch with Dalia Lamdani, a food editor in Tel Aviv, who went out of her way to share with me her vast expertise in the various cuisines of Israel. I also want to thank Shoshana Kabel and Bino Gabso, as well as all the people— taxi drivers, falafel sellers, shopkeepers, and so forth—who answered my many questions. Special thanks to my good friend Joan Nathan, who shared the results of her research on the new Israeli cuisine.

I'm grateful to Stelios Samaras, of the Greek Bank of Agricultural Seeds in Salonika, for imparting his knowledge of the chilies of the Mediterranean.

Many thanks to Isabella Oztasciyan-Bernardini, professor of Modern Greek at the University of Lecce, for help and recipes from the area around Taranto. Princess Marina Colonna, who produces the best olive oil in Molise, revealed to me some little-known hot recipes from her part of Italy. Faith Willinger explained the fine points of *peperoncini*. Many thanks to both of them, as well as to Anna Zammit in Malta. Author Clifford Wright helped me with the history of the spice trade.

Maria José Sevilla and Alicia Rios helped me to understand the various Spanish peppers and their uses, while my friend Filiz Hösukoglu, from Gaziantep, Turkey, keeps me supplied with the most delicious crushed pepper. I want to thank them all once more.

My travels in Tunisia, Morocco, and Puglia would not have been as productive if they had not been so well organized by the Oldways Preservation and Exchange Trust. I would like to express once more my gratitude to Dun Gifford, Sarah Baer-Sinnot, and Greg Drescher—although he is no longer a part of the group.

I'm continually grateful to my good friend Paula Wolfert—the food writer with the most knowledge about Mediterranean cooking—for her help and advice.

Last but not least, I want to thank my mother, Frosso Kremezi, for testing and tasting recipes, and my life's companion, Niko Kyriazidis, for his patience and understanding.

Sauces and Spreads

Fresh Tomato, Caper & Cilantro Sauce

This is my favorite summer sauce. Although chilies provide a fair amount of heat, the dominant taste is the fresh, uncooked tomatoes. This sauce is extremely versatile, good for spaghetti, bruschetta, cooked beans, and grilled meat or poultry. You must make it when tomatoes are at their best, red and meaty. But because I like this sauce so much, I freeze several batches of diced fresh summer tomatoes so I can make it even in winter.

You can make a delicious salad by mixing it with pieces of grilled crusty bread, crumbled feta cheese, and a little oregano. To make a kind of quick pizza, spread some sauce over lightly toasted pita bread, sprinkle with a little grated sharp cheese—such as pecorino or manchego—and broil for 2 to 3 minutes. For a nutritious salad or side dish, toss with cannellini beans, lentils, or a mixture of lentils and wheat berries. To make a delicious appetizer or side dish, mix with grilled eggplant and peppers.

2 pounds ripe red tomatoes

Coarse sea salt, to taste

2–3 garlic cloves, minced

½ cup extra-virgin olive oil

3 tablespoons capers, preferably preserved in salt (see Mail-Order Sources), rinsed well and chopped

2–6 fresh jalapeños, preferably red, finely chopped

⅔ cup chopped cilantro

½ cup chopped flat-leaf parsley

Dip the tomatoes in boiling water for 20 to 30 seconds, remove and place in cold water until cooled, and peel. Cut out the stem, halve, and squeeze each half to get rid of most of the seeds, then chop.

Transfer the chopped tomatoes to a colander, sprinkle with some salt, and let drain for at least 15 to 30 minutes. (Save the liquid for another use; it is very tasty.)

About 30 minutes before serving, mix the garlic with the olive oil, capers, chilies, and half the cilantro and parsley in a bowl. Just before serving, add the tomatoes to the olive oil mixture, toss thoroughly, and taste to adjust the seasoning. Mix with just-cooked spaghetti or use any way you like. Sprinkle with the rest of the chopped cilantro and parsley and serve.

Makes about 2 1/2 cups sauce,
enough for 1 pound spaghetti.

Tomato, Pepper & Onion Relish

This lovely red, hot, and densely flavored spread should be prepared when peppers and tomatoes are in season. But you can also make it with good-quality canned tomatoes fortified with 5 or 6 chopped sun-dried tomatoes added at the last minute.

To serve as an appetizer, spread on toasted crusty bread. Or spoon on baked potatoes or grilled lean chicken or fish.

3 medium red bell peppers

1 medium yellow or green bell pepper

4 pounds ripe red tomatoes

Coarse sea salt

1/3 cup extra-virgin olive oil

2 large onions, coarsely chopped

3–6 fresh red chilies, minced, or 3–6
  teaspoons Aleppo pepper
  (see Mail-Order Sources)

3 garlic cloves, minced

4 tablespoons capers, preferably
  preserved in salt (see Mail-
  Order Sources), rinsed
  well and chopped

1 large bunch cilantro
  or flat-leaf parsley,
  chopped

Black pepper

Roast the bell peppers
under the broiler or
directly on a gas burner until
black and blistery. Place in a colander, cover with aluminum foil, and let
drain for 2 minutes.

Cut the tomatoes in half and grate as
described on page 97.

In a skillet, warm half the olive oil and
sauté the onions until they start to turn
light golden brown, about 15 minutes. Add
the chilies and stir for 1 minute more. Stir
in the garlic and remove from the heat.

Turn the contents of the skillet into a
fine strainer and set over a bowl to collect
the oil. Wipe the skillet with paper towels
and pour the olive oil back into it. Add
the tomatoes and cook over high heat,
stirring often, for 8 to 10 minutes, until
nearly all their liquid has evaporated.
Let cool.

Peel the grilled peppers,
remove the seeds,
and chop the flesh
finely.

Place the
onion-chili mix-
ture in a nonreac-
tive bowl and add the
tomatoes, peppers, capers,
rest of the olive oil, and
most of the chopped
cilantro, setting aside 1 to 2
tablespoons for decoration.
Taste and adjust the seasoning with salt
and pepper.

Let stand in the refrigerator for at least
3 hours or overnight, then sprinkle with
cilantro and serve.

Serves 6.

Taratouri (Cypriot Yogurt, Cucumber & Mint Sauce)

When you burn your mouth eating very hot and spicy food, yogurt is the ideal food to soothe you; water and wine will just spread the heat further. Taratouri is similar to the yogurt sauces found all around the Mediterranean. Most of them—such as the Turkish *caçik* and the Greek *tzatziki*—contain lots of garlic and either fresh dill or fresh mint. This Cypriot version is very refreshing and can be a welcome accompaniment to chili-flavored dishes without overpowering them with a strong, garlicky flavor.

Serve Taratouri as an accompaniment to spicy meat or fish dishes, grilled vegetables, stews, or soups.

3 cups thick sheep's milk yogurt, or about 4 cups plain yogurt, drained for 1 hour (see page 103)

1 medium cucumber, peeled, grated, and drained in a colander

3–4 teaspoons dried mint (see Note)

Salt and white pepper, to taste

½ cup chopped cilantro

In a bowl, mix the yogurt with the cucumber and mint. Season to taste with salt and pepper. Let stand for 2 to 3 hours in the refrigerator. Add the cilantro and serve.

Makes about 4½ cups.

VARIATION: You can serve Taratouri as a dip with crudités or grilled pita wedges if you add 2 or 3 minced fresh chilies to the basic recipe. If you are limiting your consumption of fat, you can also make chili Taratouri with nonfat yogurt and use it as a sauce for raw or steamed vegetables.

NOTE: If dried mint is not available, you can substitute ½ cup of chopped fresh mint, but the flavor won't be the same.

Pesto with Cilantro, Arugula & Parsley

This very fragrant herb mixture is not a modern invention. The Roman author Columella, who lived in the first century A.D., describes a pesto-like blend including these herbs with some that are not often used today, such as rue and pennyroyal. The herbs were blended with scallions, salted cheese, and peppered vinegar; the latter was very popular in Roman times. Pepper, transported from India, was extremely expensive, but it was used in abundance in Imperial Rome in both sweet and savory dishes.

I came across this recipe while reading Joan P. Alcock's essay, "Flavorings in Roman Culinary Taste," delivered during the *1992 Oxford Symposium on Food and Cookery.*

In some variations of the basic pesto, Columella adds walnuts or pine nuts and gives directions to pound the ingredients in a mortar and store the resulting paste in a clay dish topped with olive oil, much as we do today. In my version I have added fresh chilies along with fragrant black pepper.

Serve as an appetizer with fresh crusty bread or crackers. Serve with spaghetti—as you would basil pesto—drizzling the freshly cooked pasta with some extra-virgin olive oil. This pesto is also good with steamed, grilled, or fried vegetables or fish, or added to vegetable, meat, or fish soups.

2 cups coarsely chopped parsley
1 cup coarsely chopped cilantro
1 cup coarsely chopped arugula
4 scallions, white part plus 2 inches
*   of green*
½ cup lightly toasted pine nuts
1 teaspoon freshly ground black pepper

2–4 small fresh green chilies, seeded,
*   or to taste*
3–4 tablespoons balsamic vinegar
½ cup grated pecorino cheese
4 tablespoons extra-virgin olive oil,
*   plus more to top the jar*
Salt, to taste

Place the parsley, cilantro, arugula, scallions, pine nuts, pepper, chilies, vinegar, and cheese in a blender or food processor in batches, and pulse, scraping the sides of the bowl frequently, until you obtain a homogeneous paste. Add the olive oil and process until it is mixed. Season with salt if necessary. Place in a bowl and top with more olive oil.

Refrigerate for 2 to 3 hours before serving. Unfortunately, this pesto doesn't keep for more than 2 to 3 days.

Makes 1 1/2 cups.

Yogurt Sauce with Hot Paprika & Scallions

Hot and sweet peppers were introduced to Hungary by the Ottoman Turks in the 16th century. And although sweet paprika is more common in the West, in the Middle East hot paprika—paprika *harif* as it is called in Israel—is the basic hot seasoning used.

In a dish called *cilbir* the Turks serve a version of this simple and delicious sauce with poached eggs, according to Claudia Roden's classic *New Book of Middle Eastern Food*. In Claudia's version the mild paprika is warmed in butter and poured over the yogurt-covered poached eggs.

Serve with poached eggs, steamed vegetables, or baked potatoes. Present as a dip with crudités or toasted pita bread. It is also delicious with Falafel (see page 74) or fried vegetables.

2–3 tablespoons olive oil
1 cup chopped scallions
1 ½–4 teaspoons hot paprika,
    preferably Turkish
1 ½ cups thick yogurt, drained
    (see page 103)
½ teaspoon salt, or to taste
Chopped cilantro or parsley,
    to decorate

Warm the oil in a skillet and sauté the scallions until soft, 2 to 3 minutes. Add the paprika, stir once, and remove from the heat. Let cool completely.

In a bowl, beat the yogurt with the scallion mixture. Add salt and taste to adjust seasoning with more salt or paprika. Refrigerate for 2 to 3 hours before serving.

Remove from the refrigerator, decorate with chopped cilantro or parsley, and serve.
Makes 1 ⅔ cups.

Zhug (Hot Yemenite Sauce)

Zhug (which is also called *zhoug*) is the hot condiment of choice in Israel. You will find it made with green or red chilies in falafel stands and in the kebab restaurants that serve *shawarma*—vertically skewered pieces of meat—accompanied by many different salads, spreads, relishes, and freshly baked pita bread.

Zhug was brought to Israel by Yemenite Jews. It is made with fresh chilies, garlic, and cardamom. It is very hot, so you should start with only a tiny amount. Mixed with soaked and ground fenugreek, it becomes Hilbeh (page 22). I prefer Zhug made from green chilies, which sets it apart from the mostly red hot sauces of North Africa.

You can add a little Zhug to soups, pasta, and bean dishes, or serve it as a condiment with Falafel (page 74) or fried vegetables. Or, you can mix with yogurt to make a delicious hot dip, or add a little to salad dressings. To make a delicious low-fat sauce or dip for vegetables, mix it with nonfat yogurt.

10–14 fresh green chilies, seeded and coarsely chopped

1 teaspoon sea salt

8–9 garlic cloves, coarsely chopped

1 teaspoon freshly ground caraway seeds

1 teaspoon freshly ground cumin seeds

1/2 –1 teaspoon freshly ground green cardamom seeds

2/3 cup coarsely chopped cilantro

1 teaspoon freshly ground black pepper

2–4 teaspoons fresh lemon juice

Place the chilies, salt, garlic, caraway, cumin, cardamom, cilantro, pepper, and lemon juice in the bowl of a food processor or in a blender and pulse several times until you get a smooth paste. You will have to scrape down all the bits and pieces that stick to the sides of the bowl.

Pack in a jar, screw on the lid, and store in the refrigerator. Zhug will keep for 1 to 2 weeks. You can also freeze it, but it will lose some of its garlicky flavor.

Makes about 1 cup.

Hilbeh (Yemenite Hot Relish with Fenugreek)

This is another Yemenite specialty I first tasted in Israel. The commercial version—without herbs or *zhug*—had a strange, bitter taste and an unappealing light brown color. But the real thing was a revelation. Shoshana Kabel—a very lively, beautiful, second-generation Yemeni woman who is eager to preserve the traditions of her homeland—taught me the right way to make Hilbeh.

I was unfamiliar with the taste of fenugreek, which cannot be found in Greece, although—ironically—its Latin name means "Greek hay." Ancient Greeks called it *telis* and used it to treat headaches and as an aphrodisiac. Fenugreek is technically not a spice—it's a legume that contains protein and minerals, which makes it very important for vegetarians.

In this sauce, the jelly-like fenugreek pulp is not used as a flavoring itself, but as a means to dilute the fiery taste of the *zhug*. You must soak it for 3 days before starting this recipe.

Use Hilbeh to flavor soups or spread it on flatbread dough just before baking to make delicious, chili-scented pitas. Serve as a dip for pitas, crackers, or crudités, and use as a relish with Falafel (page 74) or fried vegetables. Hilbeh is also very good with grilled fish.

¹/₄ cup fenugreek seeds
1 cup finely chopped parsley
3–4 scallions, chopped
2–3 shoots fresh green garlic, chopped, or
    1–2 garlic cloves, minced
1 cup chopped cilantro
4–6 tablespoons Zhug (page 20)

Soak the fenugreek in 2 to 3 cups water for 3 days. The water should be changed twice each day, and the seeds rinsed in a strainer under running water before using. The fenugreek will have swollen and lost most of its dark color and bitter taste. Place in a blender or food processor, add about ⅔ cup water, and process for 1 to 2 minutes to get a thick, gluelike paste. If it is too thick, add a little more water. Place in a bowl, cover, and refrigerate for 2 to 3 hours, until thoroughly chilled.

Place the cold fenugreek pulp in the bowl of the food processor, add another cup of water, and process for about 3 minutes. (Although Shoshana insisted that from this point the beating should be done by hand, I achieved excellent results with a food processor.) Add about ½ cup water and process another minute. The mixture should be frothy and thick, like stiffly beaten egg whites.

Transfer to a jar, cover, and refrigerate until you are ready to serve. The fenugreek mixture keeps well for about 2 weeks, and you can also freeze it. Just before serving, mix with the parsley, scallions, garlic, and cilantro and 2 to 3 teaspoons *zhug* for each cup of fenugreek pulp, according to your taste.

Makes about 3 ½ cups.

Chili & Orange Vinaigrette

I was inspired to use orange in this spicy vinaigrette sauce by Roger Vergé's recipe for "Beets with Orange and Almonds," one of the many delicious recipes in his book *Vegetables in the French Style*. I think that the combination of orange, chilies, and mustard seeds works very well. Serve with a green salad, beets, or hot or cold steamed vegetables, especially broccoli.

2 tablespoons fresh orange juice

2 tablespoons fresh lemon juice

1 teaspoon white mustard seeds, or ½
   teaspoon dry mustard

3–4 tablespoons fruity extra-virgin olive oil

2 tablespoons chopped fresh chili, or to taste

Salt and freshly ground black pepper, to taste

2–3 tablespoons toasted pine nuts

2 tablespoons orange zest

Mix the orange and lemon juices with the mustard and olive oil. Beat to combine. Add the chili and some salt and black pepper. Taste and adjust the seasoning.

Pour over a salad or steamed vegetables, sprinkle with the pine nuts and orange zest, and toss thoroughly.

Makes about ⅓ cup.

Laban (Middle Eastern Yogurt Sauce)

This is the basic recipe for a versatile warm yogurt sauce served with meat, vegetables, rice, bulgur, and so forth.

2 cups thick yogurt, drained
   (see page 103)

1 tablespoon cornstarch, dissolved
   in 2 tablespoons cold water

Salt, to taste

Transfer the yogurt to a medium saucepan, add the cornstarch mixture,

and stir over medium heat until it comes to a boil. Season with salt and serve.

Makes about 1½ cups.

VARIATION: Add 2 heaping tablespoons chopped dill, parsley, or cilantro, or any other herb. You can also make the sauce spicy by adding a chopped half of a fresh chili.

Appetizers, Soups, Salads

Missir (Macerated Salad)

This delicious salad is left to macerate overnight with coarse salt, lemon juice, and some chopped fresh chilies, which give it a delicious spicy zing. It is one of the appetizers served in a small, informal restaurant called Doctor Chakchouka, in Jaffa, the picturesque historic district of Tel Aviv. Bino Gabso, the restaurant's owner, serves Libyan Jewish food, based on his mother's recipes.

Add as many chilies as you like, according to how hot you want the salad. It is not necessary to add olive oil—this salad is just as tasty without it.

1 small, tender green cabbage,
   coarsely shredded
1 large green bell pepper, seeded
   and coarsely diced
1 large red bell pepper, seeded
   and coarsely diced
2 cups tender cauliflower florets
3–4 medium carrots, thinly sliced
1 daikon or 3–4 young turnips, thinly sliced
3–6 fresh green chilies, seeded and
   thinly sliced
1 ½ teaspoons coarse sea salt
3 tablespoons fresh lemon juice,
   or more to taste
3 tablespoons extra-virgin olive oil (optional)

Place the cabbage, bell peppers, cauliflower, carrots, daikon, and chilies in a large bowl, sprinkle with the salt, and toss thoroughly with your hands for 1 minute. (Wear rubber gloves if chilies irritate your skin.) Add the lemon juice, toss a few more times, cover with plastic wrap, and refrigerate for 4 to 5 hours or overnight.

Just before serving, toss once more, discard most of the accumulated juices, and taste. Adjust the seasoning by adding a little more lemon juice and some olive oil, if you like.

Serves 6 to 8.

Yogurt, Spinach & Parsley Salad with Pine Nuts

Recipes that combine spinach with yogurt are found all around the Mediterranean. This is my adaptation of an Armenian recipe to which I added chilies. Instead of serving it on the traditional pita bread of the Middle East, I prefer to pair it with toasted whole wheat or multigrain bread, rubbed with a cut clove of garlic. Serve this as an appetizer on toast points, or as a side dish with poached or grilled fish or chicken.

1 1/2 pounds spinach leaves, chopped
1 cup chopped flat-leaf parsley
3 cups thick yogurt (see page 103)
1 garlic clove, minced
1–2 fresh green chilies, finely chopped
Salt and freshly ground black pepper, to taste
1/3 cup toasted pine nuts

Place the spinach in a saucepan over high heat, cover, and let it wilt without adding more water than what is left on the leaves after washing. It needs only 2 to 3 minutes. Toss once or twice while cooking and be careful not to let it burn. Remove from the heat, place in a colander, and let the spinach cool and drain. Press with your hands to remove as much liquid as possible. Chop finely.

In a bowl, combine the spinach with the parsley, yogurt, garlic, and chilies, stirring well. Add a little salt and taste. Adjust seasoning with more salt and a little black pepper. Cover and refrigerate for at least 3 hours or overnight.

Spread on toast points, sprinkle with pine nuts, and serve as an appetizer, or transfer to a serving dish, sprinkle with pine nuts, and present as a side dish.

Makes about 3 cups.

Preserved Lemons with Hot Paprika

In Israel, small hot preserved lemquats, reddish from paprika and drizzled with some fruity olive oil, are part of nearly all appetizer spreads. If you cannot find lemquats or small, thin-skinned lemons, use lemon slices (see Note), which are also served throughout the Middle East.

Serve as an appetizer or as an accompaniment to steamed vegetable salads—they are particularly good in potato salads, or add to stews and stuffings. They are an ideal complement for cold meats and smoked or grilled fish.

1 1/2 pounds small lemons
   (preferably Meyer lemons)
About 1/4 cup coarse sea salt
2–3 tablespoons hot paprika,
   preferably Hungarian
1/2 teaspoon turmeric
Juice of 4–5 lemons
About 1/3 cup olive oil

With a very sharp knife, cut the lemons into quarters lengthwise without detaching the pieces completely at the stem end. Sprinkle salt and a little paprika inside each lemon and place in a 1-quart jar. Press down on the lemons to fit as many in the jar as possible. Refrigerate for 2 to 3 days. The lemons will give off a lot of juice.

Press the lemons in the jar to extract as much juice as possible. Sprinkle with the turmeric and add more lemon juice to cover the lemons. Top with 1 inch of olive oil, close the jar, and keep in the refrigerator for 4 weeks before using.

To use, remove the lemons you need, wash under running water, drizzle with olive oil, and serve or use as you wish.

Makes 1 quart.

NOTE: Instead of whole lemons, you can preserve lemon slices. Place them in layers in a bowl, sprinkling salt and paprika over each layer. Let stand for 1 to 2 days, then place in a jar, pouring in their juice and more lemon juice to almost cover. Top with olive oil and let stand for about 2 weeks before serving, as described above.

Hummus with Chickpeas, Garlic & Chilies

Chickpeas play a very important role in the cooking of all Mediterranean countries. Cooks in Palermo, Sicily, prepare a flat cake of chickpea flour, cut it in slices, and fry it to serve as an appetizer. In Egypt and the Middle East, Falafel (fried chickpea patties, see page 74) and *hummus bi tahini* (chickpeas with sesame paste) are favorite dishes.

In the colorful shops of the Carmel market in Tel Aviv, mountains of hummus are displayed between layers of whole, cooked chickpeas, sprinkled with paprika and some parsley. In restaurants, whole chickpeas are often served in the center of a plate of hummus. This gave me the idea to combine two different chickpea dishes: the extremely tasty *ceci all'aglio* (chickpeas with garlic), a traditional dish from Calabria—the southwestern tip of the Italian mainland—and *hummus bi tahini*, a ubiquitous feature of Middle Eastern cuisine. Serve accompanied with fresh or toasted pita bread, or with fresh country bread.

2 cups dried chickpeas, soaked in water overnight, or 3 1/2 cups canned

4 tablespoons olive oil, plus more fruity extra-virgin olive oil to drizzle over hummus

5 garlic cloves, minced

2–5 teaspoons Aleppo pepper (see Mail-Order Sources) or red pepper flakes

Sea salt, to taste

1 1/2–2 teaspoons hot Hungarian paprika

1/2–2/3 cup tahini

2–3 tablespoons fresh lemon juice

1/2–1 teaspoon freshly ground cumin (optional)

3 tablespoons chopped parsley

If you are using dried chickpeas, drain them and rinse them with cold water. Place in a pot, cover with water, and bring to a boil. Lower the heat to medium and cook the chickpeas for about 1 1/2 hours, or until tender, adding more water if needed during the cooking. Drain.

In a deep skillet, warm the olive oil and sauté half the garlic with the red pepper flakes until it starts to color, about 1 minute. Add 1 1/2 cups of the cooked or canned and drained chickpeas and some salt. Sauté until all liquid has evaporated.

Taste, adjust the seasoning, and set aside or refrigerate, covered, for up to 5 days.

In a food processor or blender, process the rest of the chickpeas to obtain a smooth paste. Add the rest of the garlic, a little paprika, the tahini, 2 tablespoons of lemon juice, salt, and the cumin. Process to mix thoroughly, taste, and adjust the seasoning.

You can store the hummus, covered, in the refrigerator for about 5 days.

When you are about to serve, transfer the hummus to a shallow bowl. Make a well in the center and add the chickpeas with garlic. Sprinkle with paprika and parsley and serve at room temperature.
Serves 6 to 8.

Eggplant Stuffed with Chili, Parsley & Garlic

This is my mother's adaptation of a traditional Mediterranean appetizer. In the original version the small eggplants, stuffed with a mixture of chilies, garlic, and celery, are pickled in vinegar. In this version the eggplants are blanched, stuffed, and then drizzled with a vinaigrette. The resulting appetizer has a much smoother and sweeter taste that is complemented by the pungent garlic-chili filling and the vinaigrette.

You can serve them as an appetizer, but they also make a great accompaniment to grilled fish or poultry.

2 pounds small eggplants, each about 3 inches long
Coarse sea salt, to taste
2 cups chopped parsley, preferably flat-leaf
3–4 garlic cloves, chopped
3–6 fresh green chilies, seeded and finely chopped
1/2 cup good-quality red wine vinegar or sherry vinegar
3 tablespoons balsamic vinegar
1/2 cup extra-virgin olive oil

Cut the stem from each eggplant and wash and dry them. Make a slash lengthwise, starting $\frac{1}{3}$ inch from the stem and finishing $\frac{1}{3}$ inch from the tip of each eggplant. Sprinkle a fair amount of salt inside the cut. Let the eggplants stand for about 1 hour.

Bring about 4 quarts of water to a boil in a large pot. Add about 3 tablespoons salt and drop the eggplants into the pot. Let them boil, uncovered, 20 to 30 minutes, until tender when pierced with a fork. Remove the eggplants from the pot with a slotted spoon, place in a colander, and let drain for several hours or overnight.

In a bowl mix the parsley, garlic, and chilies with 1 to 2 teaspoons salt. Toss well with your fingers to wilt the parsley. Place the drained eggplants in a glass or clay dish that holds them in one layer. Stuff the slash in each eggplant with the parsley mixture. Mix the vinegars and olive oil and pour over the stuffed eggplants.

Cover and refrigerate for at least one day before serving. The eggplants keep refrigerated for about 3 weeks.

Makes about 24 little eggplants, to serve 10 to 12 as an appetizer.

North African Zucchini Salad with Garlic, Chili Paste & Caraway

Mashed vegetables such as carrots and zucchini are dressed with a spicy sauce and served as appetizers in Tunisia and other North African countries. The zucchini available in the Eastern Mediterranean are light green and are juicier and tastier than the dark green zucchini available in Northern Europe and North America. You can sometimes find these at farmers' markets where they are called Middle Eastern zucchini, or you can grow them in your garden. The resulting salad will taste even better.

Serve as an accompaniment to grilled meat, poultry, or fish. You can make this salad as hot as you like by adding more chili paste, especially if the dishes you are serving it with are mild.

9–10 medium zucchini, steamed or boiled in
    salted water until tender
1 tablespoon balsamic vinegar
1 tablespoon good-quality red wine vinegar
2 tablespoons extra-virgin olive oil
1 garlic clove, finely minced

3–5 teaspoons Red Pepper Paste (page 99),
    or 2–3 teaspoons Harissa (page 100)
1 ½ teaspoons freshly ground caraway seeds
Sea salt, to taste
Some Kalamata olives, to decorate
2 hard-cooked eggs, quartered (optional)

Mash the cooked zucchini with a fork and place in a fine strainer. Let it drain for 20–30 minutes, until most of the liquid has run off.

Mix the vinegars, olive oil, garlic, red pepper paste, caraway, and salt in a small bowl. Place the mashed zucchini in a deep dish and pour the vinaigrette over it. Mix well, taste, and adjust the seasoning. Cover and refrigerate for 2 to 3 hours or overnight.

Serve decorated with olives and quartered hard-cooked eggs, if you like.

Serves 4 to 6.

VARIATION: You can substitute butternut squash or any other winter squash for the zucchini. A similar salad can be made with cooked carrots or cauliflower.

Increase the amount of vinegar if the vegetables are very sweet. In Israel, I tasted a delicious squash and mashed potato salad dressed the same way.

Green Beans with Garlic, Chili, Vinegar, Caraway & Cilantro

This marvelously simple and delicious vegetable dish is tasty even if you make it with frozen green beans. It comes from Algeria, the North African country with the most fiery version of couscous.

You can serve these beans as a salad, appetizer, side dish, or light lunch, accompanied by Monterey Jack, mozzarella, manouri, or any other soft cheese, with plenty of fresh crusty bread to dip in the delicious sauce.

In its original form, the sauce was made with regular vinegar, but sherry or balsamic vinegar makes it taste better. Although this dish can be served cold, it is far better warm.

1 pound green beans, cleaned, blanched in
    salted water, and drained
3–4 tablespoons extra-virgin olive oil
3–5 fresh green chilies, minced
2–3 garlic cloves, minced
⅔ teaspoon caraway seeds
1–2 tablespoons excellent-quality vinegar,
    preferably sherry or balsamic
Salt, to taste
Freshly ground black pepper
4 tablespoons chopped cilantro

Cut the beans into 2-inch pieces. In a sauté pan or deep skillet, warm the olive oil and sauté the chilies for 1 to 2 minutes, until wilted. Add the garlic and caraway, lower the heat, and stir a few times without let-ting the garlic color. Add the beans and toss well to coat with the olive oil mixture. Cook for 3 to 4 minutes, until all the liquid has evaporated. When they start to sizzle, add half the vinegar and season with salt. Remove from the heat, taste, and adjust the seasoning with more vinegar, salt, and freshly ground pepper. Sprinkle with the cilantro and serve immediately.

Serves 4 as a side dish or appetizer, and 2 as a light lunch.

VARIATION: Substitute fresh shelled and peeled fava beans for the green beans. Fresh, young fava beans need no blanch-ing. You may want to cook them in the olive oil mixture a little longer, adding 2 to 3 tablespoons of water.

Eggplant Salad with Yogurt & Cilantro

Here is one more eggplant salad from the endless variety that you will find in every Mediterranean country. This one is quite hot, but the pungent taste is moderated by the soothing yogurt and chopped tomato. I first tasted it in a taverna in Nicosia, Cyprus, more than fifteen years ago. The cook told me that it was a Lebanese recipe.

During that trip I first tasted cilantro, which Cypriots add to all salads and numerous other dishes. I loved it, and because it was not yet available in Athens, I started to grow it in pots outside my kitchen window. Serve this salad with toasted pita or fresh crusty bread.

1 large eggplant, about 1 pound or more

Salt

1/2 cup flour

3–5 tablespoons olive oil

3–6 fresh green chilies, minced

2–3 garlic cloves, minced

1–2 teaspoons balsamic vinegar,
   or more to taste

1/2 cup chopped flat-leaf parsley

1/2 cup chopped cilantro

1/2–3/4 cup thick yogurt (see page 107)

Freshly ground black pepper, to taste

1/2 cup peeled, seeded, and finely diced
   fresh tomato, drained

A few parsley sprigs, to decorate

Peel and cut the eggplant into 1/2-inch dice. Place in a colander and sprinkle with plenty of salt. Toss and let drain for about 1 hour.

Squeeze the eggplant pieces to remove more liquid, drain on paper towels, and transfer to a bowl. Add the flour and toss well to coat all the pieces.

Warm the olive oil in a heavy skillet and sauté the eggplant until golden brown, about 8 minutes. Transfer to paper towels and let cool.

Mix the chilies, garlic, half the vinegar, parsley, cilantro, and yogurt. Add the cooled eggplant cubes, toss, and taste. Adjust the seasoning with more yogurt, some freshly ground pepper, more vinegar, and salt to taste.

Place in a deep dish, make a well in the center, and fill it with the chopped tomato. Decorate with sprigs of parsley and serve.

Serves 4.

Cold Almond & Garlic Soup

I make this cold spicy soup from Spain frequently during the summer. I find its taste irresistible, especially with the bite given to it by the fresh ginger. Although the traditional *ajo blanco* served today is very mild, I'm sure that in its Medieval form it would have been much spicier.

The quality of the almonds plays a very important role in this dish. Don't use peeled almonds if you have time to peel your own (see Note). But if you have to use peeled almonds, let them soak in cold water for a couple of hours or overnight. Instead of the water the original recipe required, I use homemade chicken stock.

³/₄ cup peeled almonds

1–2 garlic cloves, halved lengthwise, sprout removed

¹/₂–1 teaspoon sea salt

1 ¹/₂ cups toasted whole-wheat or multigrain bread crumbs

3 cups defatted homemade chicken stock or excellent-quality chicken broth

5 tablespoons extra-virgin olive oil

1–2 tablespoons grated fresh ginger

2 tablespoons sherry vinegar

Freshly ground white pepper, to taste

4–8 sprigs flat-leaf parsley or cilantro

Some red and green grapes, for garnish

Place the almonds and garlic in the bowl of a food processor or blender. Add the salt and process to obtain a smooth paste.

If necessary, add a few tablespoons of water. Add the bread crumbs and a little chicken stock to the mixture. Process again for a few seconds.

Add the grated ginger, olive oil, and vinegar to the almond mixture. Process again, adding the remaining stock to obtain a creamy soup. Taste and adjust seasoning with white pepper. Transfer to a covered container.

Refrigerate for 2 to 3 hours or overnight. Stir well before serving and decorate each bowl with sprigs of parsley or cilantro and some fresh red and green grapes.

Serves 4.

NOTE: To peel the almonds, blanch them for 1 to 2 minutes, drain, and rub with your fingers to remove the skins.

Pasta e Fagioli (Pasta with Beans)

Beans are the trademark of Mediterranean peasant food. The heat in this version comes from tasty pancetta coated with red pepper flakes. You will find it in some Italian food stores, especially those that carry foods from Calabria.

Of all the different varieties of pasta, I have found that *orecchietti* ("little ears")— which are the traditional pasta of Puglia, in Southern Italy—are best suited for *pasta e fagioli*. Somehow, a bean seems to rest inside the curve of each *orecchiette*. In Puglia the dish is made with fresh homemade pasta. This recipe is my own adaptation of a dish I tasted in the *Trattoria Cucina Casareccia*, in Lecce.

2 cups fresh cranberry beans, or 1 cup dried cranberry beans soaked in water overnight

1/3 cup olive oil, plus additional to fry the pasta

1 cup chopped onion

1 teaspoon freshly minced garlic

2/3 cup (3 1/2 ounces) chopped pancetta Calabrese (pancetta coated in red pepper flakes) or ordinary pancetta or bacon

3–5 teaspoons Aleppo pepper (see Mail-Order Sources) or red pepper flakes to taste

1/2 cup dry white wine

1 1/2 cups good-quality tomato pulp

2/3 pound orecchietti

Sea salt and freshly ground black pepper, to taste

3 tablespoons chopped fresh parsley

5–6 tablespoons grated Parmesan cheese (optional)

If you are using soaked dried beans, drain them, rinse with cold water, place in a pot, cover with water, and bring to a boil. Lower the heat and simmer for about ¾ to 1 hour, until the beans are almost soft but still firm. Drain.

In a heavy pot warm the olive oil and sauté the onions for 2 to 3 minutes, until translucent. Add the garlic, the pancetta or bacon, 1 teaspoon Aleppo or pepper flakes, and the fresh or cooked beans. Sauté for another 2 minutes, until all the water has evaporated. Pour in the wine. Cook over high heat for 30 seconds, then add the tomato pulp and about 1 cup water. Bring to a boil and simmer for 30 to 45 minutes, until beans are very tender, adding water if needed. Season to taste with salt and more red pepper flakes.

Cook the pasta al dente and drain. Halfway through cooking, take about a handful of *orecchietti* out of the pot with a slotted spoon. Drain on a kitchen towel and fry in olive oil until golden and crunchy. Drain on paper towels.

Mix the cooked pasta with the bean mixture. Cover and let stand for 5 minutes. Add the fried pasta and mix well. Taste and adjust seasoning.

Serve very warm, sprinkled with parsley, Parmesan cheese, or both.

Serves 4.

Hot and Spicy Yogurt Soup

You will find variations of this simple yogurt soup all over the Middle East. I came across an old Armenian recipe for *madzoun abour* in Pascal Tchakmakian's book *100 Recettes de Cuisine Arménienne* (100 Recipes from Armenia) that included barley, while a friend's mother who comes from Pontos—an old Greek settlement on the Black Sea—makes her yogurt soup with bulgur, and calls it *arianassi*.

The basic ingredients are the same: onions, olive oil or butter, a cereal of some kind, water or stock, yogurt, and dried mint. In my version, red pepper flakes and freshly ground black pepper give the soup a bite.

3 tablespoons olive oil

1 1/2 cups chopped onions

1/2–1 teaspoon Aleppo pepper (see Mail-
     Order Sources) or red pepper flakes

1/2 cup dry white wine (optional)

4–5 cups chicken stock

1/3 cup coarse bulgur

3 tablespoons fine semolina flour

2 cups plain yogurt

2 tablespoons dried mint or 1/3 cup
     chopped fresh mint leaves

Salt and freshly ground black pepper,
     to taste

Warm the olive oil in a skillet and sauté the onions for about 4 minutes, until soft. Add the pepper flakes and turn a few times. Pour in the wine, if you are using it, and the stock and bring to a boil. Add the bulgur and semolina, stirring constantly, and simmer for 15 minutes.

In a bowl, mix the yogurt with about 1 cup of the boiling soup and stir well. Pour the mixture into the soup, stirring constantly. Add the mint, rubbing it with your fingers to break up the pieces, taste, and adjust the seasoning with salt and freshly ground black pepper. Serve very warm.

Serves 6.

Spicy North African Soup with Capers

Coriander, caraway, fiery *harissa*, garlic, and fresh lemon juice give this vegetarian soup a typically North African flavor and aroma. The capers are a very unusual addition.

1/4 cup olive oil

1 tablespoon minced garlic

1 1/2 teaspoons freshly ground
    coriander seeds

1 tablespoon freshly ground
    caraway seeds

1 teaspoon Harissa (page 100)

1 teaspoon Aleppo pepper
    (see Mail-Order Sources)
    or red pepper flakes

1 tablespoon tomato paste

1/4 cup fine semolina

1/3 cup coarse bulgur

3–4 tablespoons fresh lemon juice

1/2 cup capers preserved in salt (see
    Mail-Order Sources), rinsed very well
    under running water

1 Preserved Lemon with Hot Paprika
    (page 28), rinsed and cut in fine
    julienne (optional)

Salt, to taste

4 tablespoons chopped cilantro or parsley

Mix the olive oil with the garlic, coriander, caraway, *harissa*, and pepper flakes in a saucepan. Place over medium heat and stir to warm, without letting anything burn. Add the tomato paste and 4 to 5 cups water. Bring to a boil and add the semolina and bulgur, stirring constantly. Simmer for 10 minutes, then add the lemon juice, capers, and preserved lemon. Taste and season with salt if desired or some more preserved lemon.

Serve very warm, sprinkled with cilantro or parsley.

Serves 6.

Chicken & Onion Soup with Hilbeh

I had this soup for lunch in the home of Shoshana Kabel—a remarkable Yemenite Jewish woman—in the outskirts of Tel Aviv. She is expert in making *hilbeh* (page 22), a jelly-like fenugreek and chili sauce that is typical of Yemenite cuisine. As we were eating lunch in her kitchen, women from the neighborhood kept arriving with jars to get a little of Shoshana's *hilbeh* while bringing her their own specialties. One woman brought delicious pita bread baked with some *hilbeh* spread on it, which we devoured with our soup.

In Shoshana's version, this soup contained no pasta and was flavored with her own spice mixture. Trying to re-create it in my kitchen, I managed to achieve a very similar taste with *ras el hanout*, the traditional Moroccan spice blend (see page 96).

3 tablespoons olive oil

1 skinless and boneless chicken breast, cut into thin strips

1 skinless and boneless chicken thigh, cut into thin strips

1 cup chopped onion

2 scallions, chopped

1/2 cup dry white wine

1 1/2 quarts homemade chicken stock

1/3 cup very small pasta, such as stellini or pastina

1/2 teaspoon Ras el Hanout (page 96)

1/4 teaspoon turmeric (optional)

Pinch of saffron threads

Salt and freshly ground pepper, to taste

1/2 cup Hilbeh (page 22 and Note)

Warm the olive oil in a large saucepan. Sauté the chicken pieces until golden, 3 to 4 minutes. Remove with a slotted spoon and add the onion. Sauté for 2 minutes, until just soft, return the chicken to the pot, and pour in the wine. Let boil for 30 seconds, then pour in the stock. Bring to a boil and add the pasta, *ras el hanout*, turmeric, saffron, and some salt. Lower the heat and simmer for 10 to 15 minutes, until chicken and pasta are cooked. Taste and season with salt and a little pepper, if you need it.

Pour into soup bowls and add about a tablespoon of *hilbeh* to each one. Stir well before serving.

Serves 4–6.

NOTE: If you don't want to prepare Hilbeh, add minced green chili mixed with finely chopped cilantro and minced garlic to the soup, or add a little Zhug (page 20).

Bigilla (Maltese Dried Fava Bean Puree)

I went to great lengths to taste this traditional Maltese specialty. It is mentioned in all the local cookbooks but—as is the case in almost all countries—the simple foods of the poor have disappeared from modern restaurants. Finally, in La Maltija—a lovely small restaurant in Valletta, Malta's capital—the waiter said, "Yes, we have *bigilla*," although the appetizer was not on the menu. I was asked if I wanted it spicy and when I said "yes," I was given a small bottle of Caribbean Hot Pepper Sauce. Almost no modern cook in Valletta bothers to chop the tasty local fresh hot chilies to add to the dressing for Bigilla.

Traditionally, dried favas are cooked and mashed with their skins, so *bigilla* is brown and nutty in taste. Nevertheless, you can also make it with peeled dried favas (see Mail-Order Sources) or even with canned favas.

A very similar appetizer, called *Bissara*, is served in Egypt. It also contains a fair amount of ground cumin and dried mint (see Variation).

Serve Bigilla as an appetizer, with crackers or toasted crusty bread. Maltese bread—still baked in traditional wood-burning ovens—is wonderful.

1 ½ *cups dried fava beans, soaked in water overnight*
1 ½–3 *teaspoons Aleppo pepper (see Mail-Order Sources)*
1 *fresh jalapeño, minced*
3–4 *tablespoons red wine vinegar or sherry vinegar*
5–6 *tablespoons fruity extra-virgin olive oil*
Sea salt
1 ½–3 *teaspoons freshly minced garlic, or to taste*
1 *cup chopped fresh parsley, preferably flat-leaf, plus a few sprigs for decoration*
Freshly ground black pepper

Rinse the favas, place them in a large pot, and cover with cold water. Bring to a boil and simmer for about an hour, until they are tender—almost mushy. Drain and mash with a fork or put through a food mill, using a disk with the largest holes.

In a bowl make the sauce. Combine the Aleppo pepper, minced jalapeño, 3 tablespoons vinegar, the olive oil, and a pinch of salt. Mix well. Add the garlic and parsley, combine with the mashed favas, and mix thoroughly. Taste and adjust seasoning with more vinegar, salt, or freshly ground pepper to taste. Cover and refrigerate for at least 3 hours before serving. Decorate with sprigs of parsley.

Serves 4–6.

VARIATION: To make *Bissara*, omit the parsley, and add 1–1 ½ teaspoons freshly ground cumin and about 1 teaspoon crushed dried mint.

Spicy Tomato, Pepper, Cucumber & Parsley Salad

This is the standard salad you find in every taverna or restaurant in Istanbul. Turkish food is usually eaten with a spoon, and so is this salad—all its ingredients are finely chopped. Instead of a lemon vinaigrette, which is the usual dressing, I prefer to add a little balsamic vinegar, some orange zest, and fragrant crushed pink peppercorns to enhance the flavor. Add as much jalapeño pepper as you like, according to your taste.

Serve with any appetizer or as a side dish with meat, poultry, or fish. You can also spread it over toasted country bread for a light and delicious *crostini*.

4 medium ripe red tomatoes
½ cucumber, quartered lengthwise and finely
    sliced
1 cup tightly packed coarsely chopped
    purslane or parsley—preferably flat-leaf—
    or a combination of the two
3 tablespoons chopped fresh mint leaves
1 green bell pepper, seeded and finely diced
2–4 jalapeños, seeded and finely diced
2–3 tablespoons capers (preferably preserved
    in salt), rinsed well under running water
    and drained

SAUCE

3 tablespoons fruity extra-virgin olive oil
1 tablespoon lemon juice
1 tablespoon balsamic vinegar
2 tablespoons orange zest
2 tablespoons pink peppercorns, crushed
½–1 teaspoon Aleppo pepper
    (see Mail-Order Sources)
Salt and freshly ground black pepper to taste
1 cup cubed feta cheese (optional)
Pinch of sumac (optional; see Mail-Order
    Sources)

Cut the tomatoes in half and squeeze lightly with your hand to remove the seeds. With a very finely serrated knife, dice the tomatoes and transfer to a sieve to drain.

In a salad bowl mix the cucumber, purslane or parsley, mint, bell pepper, jalapeño, and capers. Add the tomatoes.

Mix the olive oil, lemon juice, vinegar, orange zest, pink peppercorns, and Aleppo pepper. Pour over the salad and toss. Taste and adjust seasoning with salt and pepper.

Place the feta cheese cubes on top and sprinkle with the sumac, if you are using those two ingredients. Serve immediately.

Serves 4–6.

VARIATION: By adding crumbled toasted pita or pieces of toasted whole-wheat bread, you can turn it into a delicious *mechouia*, a common Middle Eastern bread salad.

Hot Peppers Stuffed with Anchovies

This is one of the simple and delicious appetizers of southern Italy. All over the Mediterranean, hot local chilies are pickled in vinegar and served with olives or cheese in a spread of meze. But these stuffed chilies preserved in olive oil are quite different. The tasty anchovy and parsley stuffing transforms them into a special antipasto. You can use either jalapeños or Anaheim chilies, according to your taste for chilies.

Serve slices of these peppers on toasted country bread or Chickpea Bread (page 84). The preserving oil is a delicious addition to salad dressings or pasta sauces.

*10–15 jalapeños or Anaheim chilies
(as many as you can tightly fit into
a pint jar)*
*10–15 flat anchovy fillets (as many
as there are chilies)*
Bunch of flat-leaf parsley
1–2 bay leaves
1 teaspoon oregano
*1 cup or more extra-virgin olive oil,
to fill the jar*

Cut off the stem end of each chili and carefully remove the seeds. You may need to wear rubber gloves to protect your hands. Place one anchovy fillet inside each chili with 1 sprig of parsley. Squeeze as many chilies as you can into a pint jar. Add the bay leaves and oregano and fill the jar with olive oil.

Keep in the refrigerator for 4–6 weeks before serving. Take out the chilies you will consume 2–3 hours before serving.

Makes 1 pint.

NOTE: The olive oil will turn murky and semi-solid in the refrigerator.

Main Courses

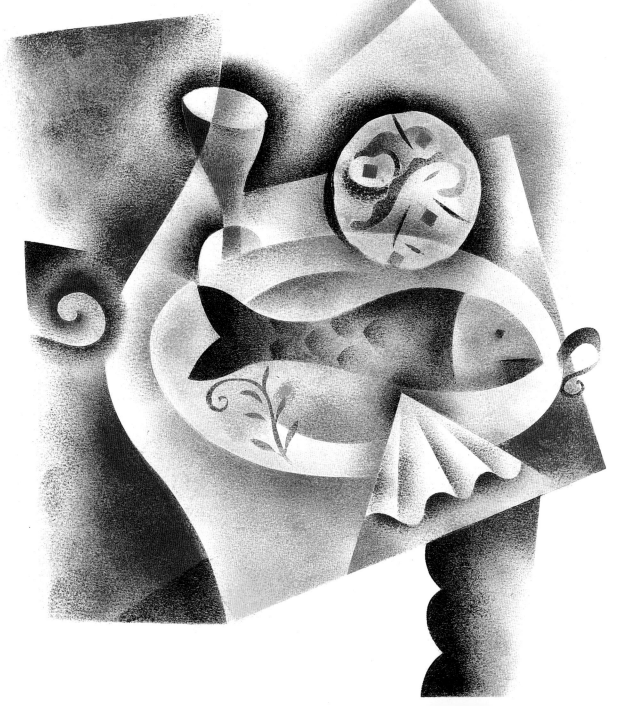

Charmoula-Marinated Grilled Tuna

A classic spicy Moroccan marinade used primarily for fish, *charmoula* is also good for meat and poultry. You will find it in many different variations, but this is my favorite. You can marinate skewered tuna chunks, salmon, or other fish, whole or filleted, in this delicious herb and spice mixture.

Serve this grilled tuna with steamed potatoes or a mixture of steamed vegetables: zucchini, carrots, green beans, and so forth, dressed in a simple vinaigrette made with lemon juice.

Charmoula can also be used as dressing for grilled or fried eggplant, zucchini, or other vegetables.

4 tuna steaks, about ½ inch thick
Sea salt
3 garlic cloves
3–5 tablespoons Harissa *(page 100) or Red Pepper Paste (page 99)*
½ cup coarsely chopped cilantro
½ cup coarsely chopped flat-leaf parsley
1 teaspoon ground cumin
1 teaspoon sweet paprika
2 tablespoons red wine vinegar
3 tablespoons balsamic vinegar
3 tablespoons olive oil
A few sprigs of parsley and lemon slices, to decorate

Wash and dry the tuna steaks and salt them lightly. Place the garlic, *harissa*, cilantro, parsley, cumin, paprika, vinegars, and olive oil in a food processor and process to obtain a paste. Rub the fish steaks on both sides with the paste and let stand for about 1 hour, covered, in the refrigerator.

Broil for 3 to 4 minutes on each side or, better, grill over charcoal.

Decorate with sprigs of parsley and slices of lemon and serve.

Serves 4.

Grilled Whole Fish in a Chili, Garlic & Mint Sauce

In Jaffa, the picturesque old city next to Tel Aviv, Margaret Victor-Tayar has a seafood restaurant specializing in Moroccan specialties prepared in her distinctive way. Her food—highly spiced and fragrant—is delicious. She is famous for her fish couscous and for her simple and delicious spicy grilled fish. The recipe that follows is my adaptation. Serve with steamed potatoes, zucchini, and carrots.

2–4 fresh green chilies, minced

1–2 garlic cloves, minced

1 teaspoon dried mint, crumbled, or 3 tablespoons chopped fresh mint leaves

2–3 tablespoons fresh lemon juice

4–5 tablespoons fruity extra-virgin olive oil

Salt, to taste

1 whole gray mullet, 1 ½–2 pounds, or any other whole fish suitable for grilling

A few grindings of black pepper

½ cup finely diced peeled and seeded fresh tomato, drained

2 tablespoons chopped fresh parsley

Mix the chilies, garlic, mint, lemon juice, and olive oil. Add a little salt and mix thoroughly, then adjust the seasonings. It should be hot. Let stand at room temperature for 30 minutes to 2 hours.

Broil the fish on both sides, or grill over a charcoal fire, until just firm, almost done, 10 to 15 minutes. Remove from the heat and cover with aluminum foil. Let stand for 5 minutes.

Uncover the fish, cut it open, and remove the central bone. Spread the fish open on a heatproof pan. Pour half the sauce over the fish, sprinkle with some pepper, and place under a very hot broiler for a few seconds to brown lightly. Remove from the oven, place the chopped tomatoes in a line down the middle between the two fish halves, sprinkle with the parsley, and serve, passing the rest of the sauce separately.

Serves 2.

Tuna Fillets Marinated in Vinegar & Pepper

This is my version of a dish I found in Rivka Levy-Mellul's *La cuisine Juive Marocaine* (Jewish Moroccan Cuisine), which contains excellent fish recipes. For Moroccan Jews, fish is the main dish on the Friday dinner table.

I think that the addition of chilies make this simple fish dish delicious. Cooked marinated tuna keeps well in the refrigerator for at least a week. It can be used in salads or reheated and served as a main course with steamed potatoes, spinach, or other vegetables.

2 thick tuna fillets, about 1 pound
⅔ cup excellent quality wine vinegar,
    preferably sherry
2 bay leaves, crumbled
3–6 fresh chilies, minced

⅓–½ teaspoon sea salt
5 tablespoons fruity extra-virgin olive oil
Freshly ground black pepper, to taste
3 tablespoons chopped parsley
1 teaspoon chopped garlic

Pour the vinegar over the fish, cover, and let marinate in the refrigerator for about 2 hours, turning once. Place the fillets in a deep nonreactive skillet or sauté pan that just holds them and pour the vinegar over them. Add the bay leaves, chilies, and salt, and bring to a boil. Add ⅓ to ½ cup water and cook over low heat for 15 to 20 minutes, turning once with a slotted spatula, until the fish is completely cooked and most of the liquid has evaporated.

Remove from the heat, drizzle with olive oil, and sprinkle with pepper, parsley, and garlic. Serve at once, or refrigerate.

Serves 2 as main dish, or 4 if added to a salad.

Fried Calamari Rings in a Spicy Coating

I remember the very tasty calamari I used to love to eat during our summer vacations in the Greek islands when I was a child. Today most of the calamari served in Greek tavernas and seaside restaurants is frozen, brought from far away.

Most of the calamari we now buy fresh or frozen has hardly any flavor, so I have developed this spicy coating, which gives it a delightful taste and crunchiness.

1 pound calamari, cleaned and
    cut into ¼-inch rings
4 tablespoons yellow cornmeal
4 tablespoons stale whole-wheat
    bread crumbs
3 tablespoons ground almonds
3–6 tablespoons Aleppo pepper (see Mail-
    Order Sources) or a combination of
    paprika and cayenne pepper
1 ½ teaspoons dried oregano
Olive and sunflower oil (half and half)
    for deep-frying
1 whole egg plus 1 egg white
Sea salt
2 tablespoons milk
Lemon wedges

Rinse the calamari rings. Mix the corn-meal, bread crumbs, almonds, Aleppo pep-per, and oregano in a plastic bag. Shake the moist calamari rings in the bag until they are covered with the coating.

Heat about 1 ½ inch of oil in a deep skillet to 350°F.

Beat the eggs with some salt and add the milk. Remove coated calamari rings from the bag one at a time with tongs, dip in the beaten egg mixture, and deep-fry in the hot oil until golden brown, 2 to 3 minutes. Do not crowd the pan, because the temperature of the oil will drop and you will end up with soggy calamari.

Transfer to a dish lined with paper towels. Sprinkle with salt and serve while very hot, accompanied by lemon wedges.

Serves 2 to 4.

Chicken with Cumin & Vinegar on a Bed of Lentils

I tasted this delicious and simple chicken dish at a dinner near Athens that featured foods from the Byzantine era. Dimitris Bliziotis, the chef of Platis Gastronomy, who cooked the dinner, described this dish to me. The recipe that follows is my own interpretation.

The combination of flavors brings to mind Roman, Byzantine, and medieval dishes, in which pepper, both black and white, was the dominant spice. It was added freely to all foods, savory and sweet.

4 skinless and boneless chicken breast halves

2 tablespoons all-purpose flour

⅓ cup olive oil

2–4 teaspoons freshly ground white pepper

½ cup sherry vinegar or good-quality red wine vinegar

1 teaspoon cornstarch

3–4 tablespoons cold chicken stock or water

½–1 teaspoon freshly ground cumin seeds

1 cup chopped onion

2 cups cooked and drained brown lentils (see Note)

Sea salt

3 tablespoons chopped flat-leaf parsley

Coat the chicken breasts with flour and shake off the excess. In a skillet, warm 2 tablespoons of the olive oil and sauté the chicken pieces on both sides until they are golden. Place on paper towels to drain.

Discard the oil from the skillet, wipe it with paper towels, and pour in 2 tablespoons fresh olive oil. Add 1 teaspoon pepper and as soon as it releases its fragrance, add the chicken and vinegar. Let boil for a few seconds. Dissolve the cornstarch in the cold chicken stock or water and add. Lower the heat and simmer for 2 to 3 minutes, until the sauce thickens and the chicken pieces are cooked through. Add the cumin and more pepper, taste, and adjust the seasoning. Remove the skillet from the heat and keep warm.

In another skillet, warm the rest of the olive oil and sauté the onion until translucent, about 5 minutes. Add the cooked lentils and stir to warm them. Season with salt and pepper, and divide the lentils among 4 plates. Place one chicken fillet on top of the lentils on each plate, pour some sauce over it, and sprinkle with parsley before serving.

Serves 4.

NOTE: Lentils don't need soaking. Wash, drain, place in a pot, and cover with cold water. Bring to a boil, lower the heat, and simmer for 20 to 30 minutes, until soft but not mushy and drain.

Lamb Tagine with Dried Figs & Sesame Seeds

Moroccan food in general is not as fiery as Algerian or Tunisian. The combination of salty, sour, and sweet tastes is its most obvious characteristic.

I loved the lamb with figs served in the restaurant Silia in Marrakech. Later I found a recipe for a similar dish in Hayat Dinia's book *La cuisine Marocaine de Rabat*. The recipe that follows is my own interpretation of this deeply flavored tagine. Serve the tagine with fresh country bread or with couscous.

⅓ *cup olive oil*

2 pounds unboned lamb shoulder and 1 pound boneless lamb shoulder, both cut into 2-inch chunks

5 garlic cloves, coarsely chopped

1½–3 teaspoons freshly ground black pepper

½–1 teaspoon Ras el Hanout (page 96)

Pinch of turmeric

Generous pinch of saffron threads

2 pounds dried figs, soaked in water for 3 hours

1 tablespoon honey

2 cinnamon sticks, 2–3 inches long

Salt and pepper, to taste

2 tablespoons red wine vinegar

3 tablespoons toasted sesame seeds

Place the olive oil in a large sauté pan and sauté the lamb over low heat until firm, about 10 minutes. Add the garlic and sauté a little longer without letting it color. Add 1 teaspoon pepper, the *ras el hanout*, turmeric, and saffron and add about 2 quarts water. Bring to a boil, lower the heat, and simmer for about 1 hour, until lamb is tender.

Meanwhile, place the figs, 2 tablespoons of their soaking liquid, the honey, and the cinnamon sticks in a different pan. Bring to a boil and cook over high heat for about 10 minutes until caramelized.

Check the lamb, which should be very tender. Season with salt and pepper.

Remove the lamb from the pan with a slotted spoon and keep covered. Add the vinegar to the pan and reduce the liquid to about 1½ cups. Add the lamb and figs to the sauce, cook for another 2 minutes, and serve, sprinkled with the toasted sesame seeds.

Serves 6.

Spicy Moussaka with Yogurt Topping

I cook this lighter and much hotter version of the ever-popular dish, moussaka, at home. It tastes much better the day after you make it, when all the flavors have had time to blend. Prepare it one day in advance, let it cool, refrigerate it, and reheat it just before serving. It is ideal for parties and you can easily double or triple the recipe.

2 large eggplants (about 1½ pounds),
    sliced lengthwise into ¼-inch slices
Sea salt
Olive oil
1 pound potatoes, peeled and sliced into
    ¼-inch slices
3 large green bell peppers, seeded, quartered
    lengthwise, and cut into 1-inch pieces
1 pound ground lean lamb
1½ cups chopped onions
3–5 teaspoons Aleppo pepper (see Mail-
    Order Sources) or 1½–3 teaspoons
    cayenne pepper, or to taste

⅓ cup red wine
½ cup dried Zante currants
1 pound ripe red tomatoes, grated (see page 97)
    or 2½ cups good-quality canned chopped
    tomatoes with their juice
8–12 grindings of black pepper, or to taste
1–2 pinches of freshly grated nutmeg
½–1 teaspoon Ras el Hanout (page 96;
    optional)
1 pound thick yogurt (see page 103) or a
    combination of 2 parts plain yogurt and
    1 part heavy cream
2 egg yolks

Salt the eggplant slices and place them in a colander. Let them drain for at least 30 minutes. Meanwhile heat about 1 inch of olive oil in a deep, heavy skillet and briefly fry the potato slices without letting them cook through. Remove with a slotted spoon and layer them on the bottom of a 9 × 12-inch glass or ceramic oven-proof dish at least 2½ inches deep (or an equivalent round or oval dish).

In the same frying oil, sauté the peppers, stirring often, until they start to color, about 10 minutes. Remove with a slotted spoon and reserve. Also reserve the frying oil.

Measure out ⅓ to ½ cup of oil and return it to the pan. Sauté the lamb in the olive oil, stirring often, for about 10 minutes, until no longer red. Add the chopped onions and continue to sauté, stirring, for another 10 minutes or until the onions become translucent. Add the Aleppo pepper and the red wine, and after the mixture boils add the currants and tomatoes. Lower the heat and simmer for about 15 minutes. Season to taste with salt and freshly ground black pepper and nutmeg, and add the Ras el Hanout if you are using it. Remove from the heat. The mixture should be quite spicy.

Wipe the eggplant slices with paper towels and place them on a baking sheet. Brush on both sides with the reserved oil, and broil until golden on both sides.

Preheat the oven to 400°F.

Arrange the eggplant slices over the potatoes. It doesn't matter if they overlap. Layer the sautéed peppers over the eggplants and top with the lamb and tomato sauce.

In a bowl, mix the yogurt with the egg yolks, stirring well. Pour over the lamb and tomato mixture. Bake for about 1 hour, or a little more, until the top starts to color and the moussaka is bubbly. Let cool completely, refrigerate, and reheat just before serving.

To reheat, place in a preheated oven at 400°F. for 20 to 30 minutes, until bubbly.

Serves 6.

Chicken Tagine with Seasonal Vegetables

Chicken or meat cooked with the vegetables of the season is a very common dish throughout the Mediterranean. In its North African version the *tagine*, as the stew is called, is spiced with chilies or harissa, and is cooked slowly in the traditional earthenware clay casserole with the conical cover, also called a tagine, over a charcoal fire.

I love to make tagine with chicken, because it cooks very quickly and keeps extremely well in the refrigerator for up to 6 days. It is even tastier the day after you make it.

Serve the tagine on its own or with couscous, but always with fresh crusty bread, which you can dip in the delicious sauce.

¼ cup olive oil

4 chicken thighs

1 ½ cup chopped onions

3–6 chopped fresh chilies

½ cup dry white wine

4 artichoke bottoms, peeled and kept in
   acidulated water

1 cup fresh fava beans or fresh peas

2 cups carrots, thinly sliced

1 ½ cup parsley, finely chopped

1–1 ½ teaspoon sea salt, or to taste

½–1 teaspoon Ras el Hanout (page 96)

2 cups water

⅔ cups chopped dill

3 tablespoons freshly squeezed lemon juice,
   or more, to taste

1 ½ teaspoons corn starch

3–4 Preserved Lemons with Hot Paprika (page
   28), rinsed and cut to eight pieces (optional)

Freshly ground black pepper

In a large sauté pan warm the olive oil and sauté the chicken pieces until golden on all sides. Transfer to a plate with a slotted spoon and add the onions to the pan. Sauté until translucent, about 2–3 minutes. Add the chili and the chicken pieces to the pan. Pour in the wine and add the artichokes, fava beans, carrots, and parsley. Add the salt and *Ras el Hanout,* pour in the water, and bring to a boil. Lower the heat, cover, and simmer for 15 to 20 minutes until chicken and vegetables are cooked. Sprinkle with half the dill and add the preserved lemons. Dilute the cornstarch in the lemon juice and pour it in the pan. Do not stir, but shake the pan to distribute. Let cook for 5 to 10 more minutes, then taste and adjust the seasoning, adding some freshly ground pepper or more lemon juice if needed.

Sprinkle with the rest of the dill just before serving.

Serves 4.

NOTE: You can substitute lamb for the chicken. I prefer to use boned meat from the leg or shoulder, cut into 2 ½–inch cubes. To make a similar stew using winter vegetables, substitute 4–5 turnips, 1 large celery root, and 1 sliced fennel bulb for the artichokes and fava beans.

Pasta with Lamb, Spinach, Cilantro & Yogurt Sauce

Some very interesting pasta dishes come from the Middle East, such as the Turkish *manti*—stuffed with meat and served with yogurt sauce—and the delicious spicy Afghani *ashak*—pasta half-circles stuffed with wild leeks and served with a very hot and spicy meat sauce and yogurt.

The cuisine of Persia, which has greatly influenced the cooking of all the countries around the eastern Mediterranean, includes many varieties of *khoresh*—meat and vegetable stews that are served with rice.

This unusual pasta dish is loosely based on a *koresh-e esfenaj* (a Persian meat and spinach stew), to which I have added Turkish hot paprika. The spicy sauce is complemented with the tart yogurt, following the Eastern tradition. Although I think the combination works much better with pasta, that doesn't mean that you cannot serve it with rice, as the Persians do.

1 ½ pounds washed spinach leaves

⅓ cup olive oil

1 pound lean ground lamb or beef

1 cup chopped onion

½ cup dry white wine

3–6 teaspoons hot paprika, preferably Turkish, or red pepper flakes

2 cups Grated Tomatoes (page 97), or good-quality chopped canned tomatoes

1 cup chopped cilantro, plus additional to sprinkle on top

Salt and freshly ground black pepper, to taste

2 cups thick yogurt (see page 103)

4–5 teaspoons cornstarch

1 pound linguine or spaghetti

Grated Parmesan cheese (optional)

Place the wet spinach leaves in a pot over high heat and cover. Toss a couple of times, until the spinach is wilted, 3 to 5 minutes. Drain in a colander, chop finely, and set aside.

In a sauté pan, warm the olive oil and add the ground lamb and the onion. Sauté, stirring often, until the lamb is no longer pink, the onion is soft, and all liquids have evaporated, about 8 minutes. Pour in the wine, stir, and add the paprika, tomatoes, and chopped spinach. Bring to a boil, lower the heat to medium, and cook for 5 minutes. Add the cilantro—reserving 3 table-spoons for decoration—and season with salt and pepper to taste. Cook for another 10 to 15 minutes, until the lamb and spinach are cooked and most of the liquid has evaporated. (You can prepare the sauce to this point well in advance. You can also refrigerate it for 2 or 3 days.)

Place the yogurt in a separate sauce-pan. Dissolve 4 teaspoons cornstarch in 3 tablespoons cold water and pour into the yogurt, stirring constantly. Place over medium heat and cook, stirring, until the yogurt thickens, about 3 minutes. If the yogurt is still watery, add another teaspoon cornstarch, dissolved in a little cold water.

Cook the pasta al dente and drain it thoroughly.

Meanwhile, reheat the spinach and meat sauce, remove from the heat, and mix with the cooked pasta. Pour the yogurt sauce over the pasta and toss thoroughly. Season to taste with salt and freshly ground pepper.

Serve immediately, sprinkled with chopped cilantro or Parmesan cheese.

Serves 4.

VARIATIONS: 1. Instead of spinach, substitute ²⁄₃ pound green beans, cut into ¹⁄₂-inch pieces, and 3 medium carrots, diced. Cook a bit longer, adding a little water if needed. 2. Substitute 5 thinly sliced leeks for the spinach.

Couscous with Beef, Almonds, Chickpeas & Vegetables

Most North African couscous dishes are prepared with butter, but the Jews of this region make their delicious couscous with olive oil. One of the tastiest versions of olive oil couscous I have tasted was served in a small, informal restaurant in Jaffa, Israel, called Dr. Chakchouka. The food served there is spicy and delicious, prepared following Libyan Jewish recipes that the owner's mother has taught the chef.

The following is my interpretation, based on Jewish Moroccan, Algerian, and Libyan couscous recipes.

²/₃ cup olive oil

2 cups coarsely chopped onions, plus 3 whole medium Spanish onions, peeled and halved

3 pounds beef, preferably shank with bones, cut into 6–8 pieces

3–5 fresh red chilies, seeded and coarsely chopped

2 medium green and 2 medium red bell peppers, seeded and quartered lengthwise

1 ¹/₂ cups chickpeas, soaked in water overnight

2–3 teaspoons Harissa (page 100)

Pinch of saffron threads

Pinch of ground ginger

1 cinnamon stick, about 3 inches long

4–5 turnips, peeled

4 medium carrots, cut into 2-inch pieces

4 medium tomatoes, peeled and grated (see page 97), or 1 ¹/₂ cups good-quality chopped canned tomatoes

1 ¹/₂–2 teaspoons sea salt, or to taste

1 cup coarsely chopped cilantro

¹/₂ pound fresh pumpkin or squash cut into 2-inch cubes

1 teaspoon freshly ground cumin seeds

2 ¹/₂ cups medium-grain couscous

1 ¹/₂ cups blanched sliced almonds, toasted

Freshly ground black pepper, to taste

In a large pot or in the bottom of a *couscoussière*, warm half the olive oil and sauté the chopped onions and the meat briefly without letting them brown, 3 to 5 minutes. Add the chilies, bell peppers, and chickpeas, cover with water, and cook for about 40 minutes, adding more water as it evaporates. Add the *harissa*, saffron, ginger, cinnamon, turnips, carrots, and tomatoes. Place the rinsed couscous in a steamer, sieve, or the top of the *couscoussière*. Steam it according to instructions.

Cook the meat and vegetables for another 40 minutes, until chickpeas and meat are almost tender. Take the couscous away from the pot, place it in a big bowl, and moisten with some of the cooking liquid and the rest of the olive oil and keep warm. Add salt, cilantro, pumpkin, and cumin to the meat mixture, plus more water to cover, and cook for another 15 to 20 minutes or until all vegetables are very tender and the meat falls from the bones.

Briefly steam the couscous to warm it, transfer it to a large serving platter, mix it with the almonds and some more cooking liquid, and taste to adjust seasoning. Keep it covered for 5 minutes. Discard the cinnamon stick, arrange the meat and vegetables on top of the couscous, and serve the sauce separately.

Serves 6 to 8.

NOTE: Algerians like to divide the broth in two and stir some more *harissa* into half of it. They serve it in two separate bowls, to allow people to add more or less chili-flavored broth to their couscous.

Ethiopian Lamb & Red Lentil Stew with Onion-Stuffed Chilies

In a tiny hole-in-the-wall restaurant near the old bus station in Tel Aviv, young Israeli soldiers of Ethiopian descent come to drink beer and enjoy a traditional Ethiopian lunch: a plate half-filled with thick red lentil paste and half with a fragrant spicy stew, simmered until the meat falls from the bones. It is seasoned with *berbere*, the traditional spice mixture of the region, which contains dried chilies, black peppercorns, ginger, cardamom, cinnamon, fenugreek, cloves, and allspice. With this dish come two fresh green chilies, which have been slitted open, seeded, and filled with chopped raw onion.

No forks or spoons are used and the food is brought to the mouth with pieces of *injera*, the delicious, pancake-like Ethiopian bread made with a sour batter of wheat flour and teff. Here is my own interpretation of this hearty and delicious dish.

2 pounds lamb with bones — shoulder, neck, or leg — cut into 4–6 pieces

2 tablespoons flour

3 tablespoons olive oil

4–5 garlic cloves, sliced

3–5 teaspoons Ethiopian Berbere (page 97)

2 tablespoons tomato paste

Sea salt, to taste

1 cup red lentils or yellow split peas

1 large white onion, coarsely chopped

8 fresh green chilies, slit and seeded

3 tablespoons chopped parsley (optional)

Remove all fat from the lamb and coat the pieces lightly with flour. Shake to discard excess. Warm the olive oil in a sauté pan and sauté the lamb until it just starts to color, about 6 minutes. Add the garlic, stir a few times, and pour in 2 to 3 cups of water. Add 3 teaspoons *berbere*, bring to a boil, lower the heat, and simmer for 40 minutes. Add the tomato paste, diluted in $\frac{1}{2}$ cup water, and the salt. Simmer for another 40 to 50 minutes, adding more water as needed, until lamb falls from the bones. Taste and adjust the seasoning with more *berbere* and salt. Cook 2 to 3 more minutes and remove from the heat. Discard the bones, and mash the lamb with a fork. You should have at least 1 ½ cups of juices with the meat. If not, add a little more water. Place back in the pan and cook for another 3 to 4 minutes, so that the lamb is coated with sauce.

While the lamb is simmering, cook the lentils. Pick over and wash them, transfer to a pot, and cover with 4 to 5 cups cold water. Bring to a boil, reduce the

heat, and simmer, stirring often, for 45 minutes to 1 hour, adding a little water during cooking if needed, until reduced to a thick paste. Season with salt and keep warm.

Mix the chopped onion with 2 to 3 teaspoons salt, toss, and let drain in a colander for at least 30 minutes. Stuff the chilies with the chopped onion.

Divide the lentils among 4 plates, placing them on one side of the plate. Place the lamb on the other side of the plate, and put 2 stuffed chilies on the side. Sprinkle with chopped parsley, if you like, and serve hot.

Serves 4.

Chicken Stuffed with Rice, Pine Nuts & Preserved Lemons

This is my interpretation of *dajaj mahshi*, a festive Palestinian dish I found in Aziz Shihab's book *A Taste of Palestine*. It is usually served to new brides and new mothers—especially mothers who give birth to sons, writes Shihab.

5 tablespoons olive oil

2 cups chopped onions

½ cup pine nuts

1 cup long-grain rice

1 cup dry white wine

1 teaspoon Ras el Hanout (page 96)

1 cinnamon stick, about 3 inches long

½ teaspoon freshly ground cumin seeds

3–5 teaspoons freshly ground black pepper, or to taste

Sea salt

¼ cup finely diced Preserved Lemons with Hot Paprika (page 28), well rinsed under warm water

1 chicken, about 3 pounds, preferably free-range

½ cup thick yogurt (see page 103)

3–5 teaspoons hot paprika, preferably Turkish

3 tablespoons chopped cilantro or parsley

In a large sauté pan, warm the olive oil and sauté the onions and pine nuts until onions are soft and pine nuts turn golden, about 4 minutes. Add the rice and sauté another 3 minutes until the rice is translucent. Pour in half the wine and 2 cups water and simmer until all liquid has evaporated, about 10 minutes. Add the *Ras el Hanout*, cinnamon, cumin, pepper, salt, and preserved lemons, stir, and taste to adjust seasoning.

Preheat the oven to 450°F.

Wash the chicken and pat dry with paper towels. Reserve the neck and giblets. Fill the cavity of the chicken loosely with rice, and close the opening with skewers or toothpicks. Don't pack in the stuffing as it will increase in volume while cooking. Keep the rest of the rice covered.

In a bowl mix the yogurt with the paprika and a little salt and baste the chicken all over with this mixture. Place chicken in a pan or ovenproof dish that will hold it leaving about 1 inch room all around. Pour the rest of the wine in the pan and add the neck and giblets. Cover with aluminum foil and bake for 1 hour. Uncover, reduce the heat to 400°F., and continue baking for another 30 to 35 minutes, until a fork inserted in the thigh lets out colorless juice.

Remove the pan from the oven and place the chicken in another dish and cover to keep warm. Transfer the rest of the rice to the pan where the chicken has cooked and toss to mix with the drippings, adding $\frac{1}{3}$ cup water. Place the chicken on top of the rice and place once more in the oven. Bake for another 20 minutes, until the rice is bubbly.

Sprinkle with parsley or cilantro and bring to the table.

Serves 4 to 5.

Bulgur Pilaf with Hot & Sweet Peppers

This is one of my favored pilafs, which I like to make on summer nights. Because it is cooked with olive oil, I can serve any leftovers cold as lunch the next day, with a salad.

You need to use large-grain bulgur for pilafs. If your local supermarket doesn't carry it, look in ethnic markets or health food stores. Hot and spicy rice and bulgur pilafs are often eaten mixed with yogurt in the Middle East. The refreshingly tart yogurt complements the spicy but sweet taste of the bulgur.

¼ cup olive oil

1 medium onion, chopped

1 large green bell pepper, diced

1 large red bell pepper, diced

3–5 teaspoons Aleppo pepper (see Mail-Order Sources) or red pepper flakes

2–3 garlic cloves, minced

1 ½ cups coarse-grain bulgur (see Mail–Order Sources)

½ cup dry white wine

2–2 ½ cups defatted chicken stock

2–3 teaspoons Red Pepper Paste (page 99; optional)

Sea salt, to taste

½ cup blanched sliced almonds

¼–½ cup pine nuts, toasted

¼ cup chopped parsley or cilantro

2 cups thick yogurt (see page 103), or plain yogurt drained for 1–2 hours (use nonfat yogurt, if you like)

In a large saucepan, warm the olive oil and sauté the onion for 3 to 5 minutes, until translucent. Add the diced peppers and sauté for another 4 minutes, until wilted. Add the pepper flakes and garlic, and stir a few times.

Wash the bulgur thoroughly under running water, until the water runs clear. Let it drain and add to the pepper mixture. Sauté for 4 to 5 minutes, stirring constantly, then add the wine. Let boil for a few seconds, then add 2 cups of stock. Add the pepper paste and stir.

Season with salt and add the almonds. Boil vigorously for 2 to 3 minutes, then lower the heat and simmer for 8 to 10 minutes. If it seems too dry, add a little more stock. Taste and adjust the seasoning.

Remove from the heat, cover the pan with a kitchen towel and the lid, and let stand for about 10 minutes. Remove the lid, fluff with a fork, add the pine nuts, and mix. Sprinkle each plate with chopped parsley and place some yogurt on the side.

Serves 4.

Pumpkin Risotto with Leeks, Chili & Cilantro

This spicy and delicious pumpkin risotto is my kind of comfort food. It was inspired by a traditional Italian dish. I love it so much that I keep batches of diced pumpkin in my freezer so that I can make it at a moment's notice. Risotto should always be made at the last minute and served the moment it has been taken off the heat. But you can sauté the vegetables several hours in advance.

3 leeks, white part and 1 inch of green part, very thinly sliced and well washed

1/3 cup olive oil

3–5 teaspoons Aleppo pepper (see Mail-Order Sources), or 2 teaspoons red pepper flakes

2 large garlic cloves, minced

1 1/2 pounds pumpkin or winter squash pulp, peeled and seeded, cut into 1/3-inch cubes

1/2 cup dry white wine

3 cups defatted chicken stock or water, or more as needed

1 1/2 cups arborio rice

Sea salt and freshly ground black pepper, to taste

2/3 cup grated Parmesan cheese

2/3 cup chopped cilantro

In a large skillet or sauté pan, sauté the leeks in the olive oil for 6 to 8 minutes, until translucent. Add the pepper, garlic, and pumpkin. Sauté until all the liquid has evaporated, 5 to 10 minutes. Pour in the wine and stir a few times. Add about 1/2 cup water and lower the heat. Let the pumpkin simmer for another 10 to 15 minutes, until tender. (You can prepare the vegetables to this point several hours in advance.)

Twenty minutes before serving, bring the stock to a very gentle boil in a medium saucepan. Keep warm. Heat the pumpkin mixture and, as it starts to boil, add the rice and stir a few times with a wooden spoon to coat with the olive oil.

Pour in about ½ cup of boiling stock and simmer, stirring constantly, adding more liquid as the rice absorbs it.

After about 15 minutes, taste the rice. It should be cooked but al dente. Season with salt and black pepper. Remove from the heat and stir in the cheese. Serve in heated soup plates, sprinkled with the cilantro.

Serves 4 to 6.

VARIATION: Instead of using all rice, you can use ⅔ cup rice and ⅔ cup coarse-grain bulgur and cook it in exactly the same way. The bulgur adds a nutty texture and taste to the risotto. But only coarse-grain bulgur will do for this dish (see Mail-Order Sources).

Chakchouka (Eggs Poached in Tomato & Chili Sauce)

This is usually served as an appetizer in the Middle East, but it can easily serve as a whole lunch or dinner. Similar to *huevos rancheros*, *chakchouka* gets its delicious flavor from the hot and fragant chilies of the Mediterranean. The best *chakchouka* I've tasted was served in a restaurant called Doctor Chakchouka, in Jaffa, Israel. The owner serves the dish in the skillet in which it is cooked and diners dip big pieces of bread into it devouring them instantly.

3 tablespoons olive oil

1 cup chopped onion

2 green bell peppers, seeded and cut into strips

2 poblanos or red bell peppers, seeded and cut into strips

4 jalapeños, seeded and cut into strips

2 cups fresh pulp from grated ripe tomatoes (see page 97) or good-quality canned tomato pulp

2–4 teaspoons Aleppo pepper (see Mail-Order Sources), or cayenne pepper to taste

Salt

6 eggs

Freshly ground black pepper to taste

In a large heavy skillet, warm the olive oil and sauté the onions and sweet peppers until soft, about 6 minutes, stirring with a wooden spoon. Add the jalapeños and tomatoes and cook until the mixture just starts to thicken, about 8 minutes. Add the Aleppo and cayenne pepper and some salt, taste, and adjust the seasoning.

Break one egg at a time into a cup or small bowl and slide it into the skillet while the tomato and pepper mixture is simmering. Cook for another 8 minutes, spooning sauce over the eggs, until they are set. Sprinkle with some freshly ground black pepper and serve.

Serves 6.

Folded Arab Pizza

I first tasted this delicious dish in a Turkish restaurant in Athens, and later found it as street food in Egypt, Israel, and Turkey. Armenians call it Armenian pizza. Claudia Roden, an expert on Middle Eastern food, told me that the dish originated in Egypt, where it is called *Lahma bi Ajeen*. In Turkey it is called *pide* or lahmacun, which is the name most commonly used throughout the Mediterranean today.

The filing is spicy and hot and always includes chopped meat—originally lamb. According to Roden, before tomatoes were introduced to the Mediterranean it contained tamarind.

Folded Arab Pizzas can be made round or oval, like the ones I tried at a market bakery in Izmir. I prefer this shape because it folds more easily. In Izmir, a seeded whole red chili was baked on top, then divided in half and enclosed in the folded pizza.

You can cut the pizza in pieces and serve as an appetizer or whole as a main course, accompanied with a mixed salad and Taratouri (Cypriot yogurt, cucumber and mint sauce, page 17). If you don't want to make your own bread dough, slice a commercial whole-wheat pita horizontally and use each half as a base to spread the filling.

DOUGH

1 teaspoon active dry yeast
1 cup whole-wheat flour
2–2 1/2 cups unbleached all-purpose flour
    or 1 cup all purpose flour and 1 1/2 cups
    bread flour

3 tablespoons olive oil
1 1/2 cups warm water, or more if needed
1 teaspoon coarse sea salt

FILLING

1/3 cup olive oil

2 cups chopped onions (1–2 large onions)

1 medium eggplant, finely diced,
    salted and left in a colander
    to drain for 30 minutes

1 medium green bell pepper, diced

1 medium red bell pepper, diced

3–5 teaspoons Aleppo Pepper (see Mail-
    Order Sources) or red pepper flakes

3/4 pound ground lean beef, lamb, or chicken

1 1/2 cup fresh grated tomatoes (see page 97)
    or diced canned tomatoes, drained

1 tablespoon tomato paste

1/2 teaspoon ground allspice
    and / or 1/2–1 teaspoon Ras el
    Hanout (page 96)

Salt, to taste

1/2 cup finely chopped parsley

1/3 cup pine nuts

Cornmeal, to spread on baking surface

In the bowl of a mixer equipped with dough hooks, place the yeast and flour. Work for a few seconds to combine. Add the olive oil and half the water and mix for about 2 minutes. Add the salt and more water and mix for another 2 minutes. The dough should be soft and slightly sticky.

Turn it out onto a lightly floured board and knead with lightly oiled hands until the dough is no longer sticky. Form into a ball, oil the bottom of a large bowl, and roll the dough into it. Cover with plastic wrap and let rise for about 1 1/2 hours, until doubled. (You can also leave the dough overnight in the refrigerator. The next day, leave it at room temperature for about 2 hours before proceeding further).

Make the filling. Warm 3 tablespoons of the olive oil in a skillet and sauté the onions until translucent, about 3 minutes. Rinse the diced eggplant under cold water, drain well on paper towels, and add to the skillet, along with the bell peppers. Sauté, stirring often, until all the vegetables are wilted, about 5 minutes. Add 2 to 3 teaspoons pepper flakes and the ground beef. Saute, stirring, until the meat is no longer red. Add the tomatoes, tomato paste, allspice or ras el hanout, and salt. Saute until almost all the juices have evaporated, about 8 minutes. Remove from the heat, add the parsley, taste, and adjust the seasoning. It should have a strong flavor.

Warm the rest of the olive oil with the remaining pepper flakes and set aside.

Place a pizza stone or a large, heavy baking sheet in the oven. Preheat the oven to 450°F.

On a lightly floured board, divide the risen dough into 8 pieces and flatten each one with your palm. Cut a 8 × 20 inch piece of parchment paper and roll out each piece of dough on it with a floured rolling pin to form an elongated oval, about 4 × 15 inches. Brush the flattened dough with the pepper and oil mixture and then spread about ½ cup of the filling evenly on each pizza, nearly covering the entire surface. Sprinkle with the pine nuts.

Sprinkle the heated pizza stone or baking sheet with cornmeal and place on it as many pizzas as it can hold. Bake for 12 to 15 minutes, until the filling sizzles and the pine nuts are golden brown. The crust should remain white and soft.

Keep the baked pizzas warm as you bake the rest. Cut each pizza in two and fold lengthwise. Wrap half in parchment paper and serve warm or at room temperature, as finger food.

Makes 8 Arab Pizzas.

Falafel

These delicious patties—also called *ta'amia*—are popular throughout the Middle East and North Africa. Although not very spicy if eaten by themselves, falafel are always served with a multitude of hot sauces and relishes.

They originated in Egypt, and Claudia Roden believes that they are a very old preparation, probably invented by the Christian Copts, who ate them during their numerous fast days when any food derived from animals was prohibited.

It is interesting to note that all the cultures who have tasted falafel have later adopted it to their own cuisine, because falafel is so delicious, nourishing, and an ideal street food. In Israel they are the convenience food of choice, and even in the Athenian supermarkets one can find packaged falafel mix. In traditional Greek cooking we have our own version of *revithokeftedes* (chickpea patties), usually prepared with cooked mashed chickpeas.

Needless to say there are as many variations of falafel as there are cooks. In Egypt fava beans are the main ingredient, but they are not used in Israel at all, as many people new to the consumption of favas may develop a severe allergic reaction to them.

To serve falafel the Middle Eastern way, cut a pita in half, open the pocket, slide 3 or 4 falafel into each pita half, add some chopped vegetables and a hot sauce like Zhug (page 20), a relish like Hilbeh (page 22), Red Pepper Paste (page 99), or tahini mixed with lemon and paprika. Or, you can serve the falafel on a plate, decorated with sprigs of parsley or cilantro. Serve a couple of hot sauces, bread, and a salad separately.

2 tablespoons olive oil

²/₃ cup chopped onion

4 garlic cloves, 2 minced and 2 sliced

2–3 fresh chilies, seeded and coarsely chopped

1 cup dried chickpeas, soaked in water
    overnight (preferably peeled)

¹/₃ cup red lentils or yellow split peas, soaked
    in water for 2–3 hours

6 tablespoons bulgur, soaked in water for 10
    minutes and drained

1 teaspoon baking powder

2–3 scallions, chopped

¹/₃ cup coarsely chopped cilantro

¹/₃ cup coarsely chopped parsley

1¹/₂–2 teaspoons freshly ground cumin seeds

1¹/₂ teaspoons sea salt, or to taste

Freshly ground black pepper, to taste

Olive oil for deep-frying

Warm the olive oil in a large skillet and sauté the onion until tender, 2 to 3 minutes. Add the minced garlic and the chilies, mix thoroughly, and remove from the heat.

Place the chickpeas, lentils, and bulgur in the bowl of a food processor and pulse to obtain a paste with the consistency of coarse semolina. Add the sautéed onion, sliced garlic, baking powder, scallions, cilantro, parsley, cumin, and some salt and pepper, and pulse to chop and incorporate into the mixture. Take tablespoons of the mixture and, wetting your hands, shape them into balls, then flatten.

Heat the oil in a deep skillet or small saucepan to 350°F. and deep-fry a few falafel at a time so the temperature of the oil won't drop, making the patties soggy. Remove with a slotted spoon after the falafel turn golden brown, 2 to 3 minutes. Drain on paper towels. Serve hot.

Makes about 35 to 40 falafel, serving 4 to 6.

NOTE: The falafel mixture can be refrigerated for 2 to 3 days, but omit the cilantro and add it only when you are ready to cook because it discolors quickly. A special gadget for shaping falafel is available at Middle Eastern markets. See Mail-Order Sources.

Spicy Rice Pasticcio with Gorgonzola

Pasticcio is a common Italian term that means "a mess." In cooking, it refers to a mixture of half-cooked pasta, rice, or polenta with eggs, cheese, vegetables, and ground meat that is baked in a mold, with or without a pastry crust. The dish is probably very old and arrived in Greece during the Middle Ages, when parts of the country were under Venetian rule. In old Greek *pasticcio* recipes, sugar and spices are freely mixed to create a very rich dish.

The following rice *pasticcio* was inspired by a recipe for *riso forte*, a peppery rice *pasticcio* included in Giuliano Bugialli's book *The Fine Art of Italian Cooking*. In *riso forte*, three kinds of cheese—Parmesan and two different kinds of pecorino—and lots of black pepper give the *pasticcio* its pronounced flavor. In my version I used Gorgonzola, an Italian blue cheese that, when mature, has a strong, almost peppery taste that complements the blandness of the rice. Fresh green chilies give the dish its heat—use more or less, according to your taste. Serve as a main dish, accompanied by a green salad.

1 cup short-grain rice, preferably arborio
Sea salt
¼ cup olive oil, and more to oil the pan
1 large green bell pepper, seeded and finely diced
2–4 fresh green chilies, seeded and chopped
1½–2 cups crumbled Gorgonzola cheese

½ cup freshly grated Parmesan cheese
3 eggs
¼ cup plus 1 tablespoon dried bread crumbs
1½ cups milk
Freshly ground black pepper, to taste
Sprigs of parsley, to decorate

Bring 8 cups of water to a boil and add the rice and some salt. Cook uncovered for about 12 minutes, until the rice starts to get soft. Drain and rinse briefly under cold water. Let drain and cool completely.

Preheat the oven to 375°F.

In a medium skillet warm the olive oil and sauté the sweet and hot peppers until wilted, 4 to 6 minutes. Place the rice in a large bowl, then add the peppers and their cooking oil along with 1½ cups crumbled Gorgonzola and the Parmesan. Stir well and add the eggs, one by one, stirring to mix them completely. Add about 3 tablespoons bread crumbs and the milk. Taste to adjust the seasoning with more Gorgonzola, salt, and pepper.

Oil a round 12 inch ring mold thoroughly and coat it with remaining bread crumbs. Pour in the rice mixture, smooth the top with a spatula, and bake for about 40 minutes, until set and golden on top. Let cool a little and unmold onto a plate. Decorate with sprigs of parsley, cut mold into wedges, and serve warm.

Serves 6 to 8.

Spaghetti all'Amatriciana with Eggplant

This is a classic chili-flavored Italian spaghetti recipe, enriched with eggplant. *Peperoncino*, the Italian term for any red-hot chili, plays an important role in this simple but delicious sauce. *Peperoncini*, like all chilies, vary greatly in heat. Add as many red chilies or red pepper flakes as you like to achieve the desired degree of heat.

1 medium eggplant, about 1 pound, peeled
in strips and cut into 1-inch cubes
Sea salt
½ cup all-purpose flour
½ cup olive oil or more as needed
1 cup chopped onion
3 garlic cloves, sliced
2–4 fresh red chilies, chopped, or 2–4
teaspoons Aleppo pepper (see Mail-Order
Sources) or red pepper flakes
½ cup dry white wine
2 cups Grated Tomatoes
(see page 97), or
good-quality diced
canned plum
tomatoes
Pinch of sugar
1 pound spaghetti
or bucatini
⅓–½ cup grated
pecorino cheese
Shavings of Parmesan cheese (optional)
3 tablespoons chopped parsley

Warm the olive oil in a large skillet, testing it with a piece of eggplant. If it sizzles, it is hot enough. Sauté the eggplant, tossing, until golden brown, about 4 minutes, adding a little more olive oil as needed. Remove with a slotted spoon and place in a colander placed in a bowl to collect the draining olive oil.

Using the remaining olive oil or the oil that has drained from the eggplants, sauté the onion in the skillet for 2 to 3 minutes, until translucent. Add the garlic and chilies and sauté for 1 minute more. Pour the wine into the skillet and cook over high heat for 30 seconds. Add the tomatoes and sugar, lower the heat, and simmer until most of the liquid has evaporated, about 20 minutes.

Cook the pasta until al dente in plenty of salted water following the instructions on the package. Drain well, transfer to a warm bowl, pour the sauce over it, and add the fried eggplant pieces and grated cheese. Toss well and taste to adjust the seasoning.

Serve sprinkled with shavings of Parmesan and chopped parsley.

Serves 4.

Sprinkle the eggplant generously with salt, toss well, and place in a colander. Let drain for at least 30 minutes. Squeeze to extract as much liquid as you can and spread over paper towels. Toss the eggplant pieces with the flour to coat well.

Pasta with Chickpeas (Cecci con la tria)

This simple and delicious dish comes from Puglia, situated on the heel of the Italian boot. All the versions I tasted were made with homemade pasta, part of which was fried to a crisp to add texture to the dish. You can also use dried pasta (see Note) or Peperoncini pasta. Make it as spicy as you like, using a combination of fresh jalapeño and black pepper, or drizzle with Chili Olive Oil (page 102), which is called *diauliciu* (the Devil's) in this region and is used to season many dishes.

1 cup chickpeas, soaked in water overnight
½ cup olive oil
1 pound homemade fettuccine (plain or with peperoncini) or commercial dried pasta
4 garlic cloves, thinly sliced
2–3 jalapeño peppers, minced
Sea salt
About 1 teaspoon cornstarch
2–3 tablespoons freshly squeezed lemon juice
Plenty of freshly ground black pepper
½ cup chopped flat-leaf parsley
Chili Olive Oil (page 102)

Cook the chickpeas in plenty of water, over low heat, for an hour or more, until tender. Drain the chickpeas, but reserve the cooking liquid.

In a large heavy skillet, warm the olive oil and fry about a quarter of the fresh pasta until crisp. Remove with a slotted spoon and drain on paper towels. (If you are using dried commercial pasta, see Note.) In the same olive oil, sauté the garlic and jalapeño for less than a minute, without letting the garlic color. Add the drained chickpeas and sauté 2 to 3 minutes more. Pour in about 1½ cup of the reserved cooking liquid, season with salt, and cook for another 3 minutes. Dilute the cornstarch in the lemon juice and add it to the skillet, stirring, until the sauce has thickened. Taste and adjust the seasoning with freshly ground pepper and more lemon juice, if necessary.

You can prepare the dish a few hours in advance up to this point.

About 20 minutes before serving, boil the pasta al dente, drain it, and add it to the simmering chickpeas. Crumble the fried pasta, add it to the skillet, mix well, and adjust the seasoning. Sprinkle with chopped parsley and serve, bringing the chili olive oil to the table so whoever wants it can drizzle some over his or her dish.

Serves 4 to 6.

NOTE: If you are using commercial dried pasta, boil a handful for 4 to 5 minutes, until it starts to soften. Drain it well on paper towels and then fry it in olive oil until crisp.

Potato "Focaccia"

In the strong dialect of Southern Italy, this delicious family dish is called *Fucazza de Petate,* as Tonio Piceci writes in his charming book *Oltre le Orecchiette,* in which he has gathered recipes from the region of Salento, in Puglia. His version contains no *peperoncini*—the particularly hot small Italian chilies—but several cooks in the region told me that they include *peperoncini* in their versions of this dish. Others insisted that chili olive oil—*Diauliciu* (the Devil's Condiment)—is often drizzled over the dish before baking to give it an extra bite. Italian *peperoncini* come in various forms and sizes and have a marvelous flavor as well as heat. Aleppo pepper is the best substitute.

3 pounds potatoes, freshly boiled and mashed

1 cup grated pecorino cheese

1/2 cup grated Parmesan cheese

4–5 tablespoons olive oil, plus more to oil
the dish

2 1/2 cups chopped onion

3–5 teaspoons Aleppo pepper (see Mail-
Order Sources), or red pepper flakes
to taste

1 dried Mediterranean bay leaf (optional)

1/3 cup dry white wine

1 cup Grated Tomatoes (see page 97) or
good-quality canned tomato pulp

2–3 tablespoons capers, preferably preserved
in salt (see Mail-Order Sources), rinsed
well under lukewarm water and drained

1/2 cup chopped, pitted small black Italian or
Kalamata olives

Sea salt

Freshly ground black pepper to taste

Chili Olive Oil (page 102; optional)

2–3 tablespoons toasted whole wheat or
multigrain bread crumbs

In a bowl, mix the mashed potatoes with
the cheeses, stirring vigorously. Warm the
olive oil in a heavy skillet and sauté the
onion for 3 to 4 minutes, until soft. Add
the Aleppo pepper, bay leaf, and wine and
stir a couple of times. Pour in the tomato
pulp and cook over medium heat for about
10 minutes, until most of the liquid has
evaporated. Add the capers and olives after
5 minutes. Discard the bay leaf, taste, and
adjust the seasoning, adding salt and some
freshly ground black pepper.

Oil a clay or glass ovenproof dish thoroughly and preheat the oven to 375°F.

Divide the potato mixture in half and
cover the bottom of the dish with one
half. Pour the tomato mixture over the
potato mixture, spreading it evenly. Cover
with the rest of the potato, pressing well
with your hands. Prick the surface with
the tines of a fork, drizzle with Chili Olive
Oil—or plain olive oil and some Aleppo
or freshly ground pepper—sprinkle with
bread crumbs, and bake for 40 to 45 minutes, until golden brown and bubbly.
Serve hot or at room temperature.

Serves 4 to 6.

Pampanella (Pork Tenderloin in Pepper Paste)

This recipe was given to me by Princess Marina Colona, who produces one of the best Italian extra virgin and lemon-scented olive oils in the hills of Molise, in southern Italy. A local trattoria called *La Carrese* serves *Pampanella* as its specialty. In many parts of southern Italy, a bowl of chopped dried *peperoncini*—the local hot red chilies—is always placed on the table, so everyone can add extra heat to all kinds of dishes. Marina told me that the region's hottest dishes have been introduced by Albanians, who emigrated there long ago. Serve *Pampanella* with French fries or with mashed potatoes.

4–5 tablespoons homemade red pepper paste (page 99) or imported (see Mail-Order Sources) or about 5 tablespoons Aleppo pepper (see Mail-Order Sources) mixed with 2 tablespoons olive oil and made into a paste
4–5 garlic cloves, chopped
Coarse sea salt
1½ pounds pork tenderloin, trimmed of all fat, cut into ⅔-inch thick medallions
2–3 tablespoons extra-virgin olive oil
Salt to taste
Vinegar, preferably Balsamic

Mix half the pepper paste, garlic, and salt. Spread the pepper mixture evenly on both sides of each pork medallion about 3 to 4 hours before grilling or the night before. Let stand, covered, in the refrigerator.

Preheat the oven to 400°F. Sprinkle the pork with half the vinegar and drizzle with the olive oil, then spread the remaining pepper paste evenly on all sides. Place in an ovenproof dish and roast for about 45 minutes, until cooked, turning once and sprinkling the remaining vinegar about midway through. Serve immediately.

Serves 4.

VARIATION: You can substitute skinless chicken breasts and turkey cutlets for pork.

Breads and Desserts

Chickpea Bread

The recipe for this delicious dense, chewy bread was given to me by Mark Furstenberg, who made real French and Mediterranean breads available in Washington, D.C., when he started the Marvelous Market. I have adapted this recipe for the home baker. The starter, although not absolutely necessary, gives the bread better taste and texture.

Chickpea Bread is an ideal accompaniment to stews and makes wonderful sandwiches. It is not hot or spicy, because it is supposed to be eaten with spicy foods. Nevertheless, if you want to serve it with a sweet cheese, such as ricotta, or with grilled vegetables, you can increase the amount of cayenne pepper and cumin.

1 ½ teaspoons active dry yeast (or 1 if you are using the starter)

1 ½ cups starter (optional; see Note)

2 cups all-purpose flour, plus more to sprinkle

1 ½ cups bread flour (see Mail-Order Sources)

½ cup barley flour (see Mail-Order Sources)

1 ½ teaspoons sea salt

½ teaspoon freshly ground cumin

½ teaspoon cayenne pepper, or to taste

½ cup plus 1 tablespoon cooked dry chickpeas (see page 29), or canned chickpeas, drained

Mix the yeast with ¼ cup warm water in a bowl. Stir until creamy and let stand for 10 minutes, until bubbles form on its sur-face. Mix with the starter, if you are using it, and stir vigorously.

In the bowl of a food processor fitted with dough hooks, add the flours, salt, and spices. Pulse the motor to mix. With the motor running, add the yeast mixture, 1 ½ cups water, and the chickpeas. Process for 3 minutes, adding a little more water if needed, to form a soft, slightly sticky dough.

Lightly flour a working surface, transfer the dough onto it and sprinkle it with flour. Knead the dough briefly with your hands. Form into a ball, oil a large bowl, and place the dough in it, turning to oil all over.

Let stand for about 1 ¼ hours, until it has doubled in size.

Turn again onto the floured working surface, divide in 4 and shape each into a ball. Cover with a moist towel or plastic wrap and let stand for 30 minutes. Using a plate, preferably one with ridges in the bottom, push the dough down to form disks.

Let rest, covered, for another 30 minutes. Meanwhile line the oven rack with unglazed tiles or a baking stone and preheat the oven to 500°F.

Sprinkle the dough with flour, place it on the stone, and bake for 20 to 25 minutes, until well browned.

Makes 4 flatbreads.

NOTE: One day before baking, make the starter: In a 4-quart bowl, mix ¼ teaspoon active dry yeast with ¼ cup warm water. Stir well and gradually add 1 ½ cups all-purpose flour and 1 cup cold water. Mix well until smooth, cover, and let stand at room temperature for 24 to 48 hours. The mixture will triple in size and become bubbly. Use as much as needed, and keep the rest covered in the refrigerator for future use. It will keep for more than a year. Take out and add about ½ cup flour and 2 to 3 tablespoons water every 3 to 4 weeks to feed it.

Hot & Sweet Cheese Pitas

These delicious pitas are inspired by two simple country desserts, one from Sfakia—a mountainous village in southwestern Crete. It is particularly loved in Chanea, the beautiful once-Venetian city on the northern coast of western Crete. These pitas are filled with fresh *anthotyro* or *mizythra*, the ricotta-like fresh cheeses of the area. The other pita comes from Astypalaia, another Greek island. People there make little deep-fried turnovers filled with spicy *kopanisti,* the local strong peppery blue cheese—similar to the *ricotta forte* of southern Italy—and serve them drizzled with the region's thyme-scented honey.

You can make Hot-sweet Cheese Pitas with *ricotta* or use well-drained farmer's or cottage cheese, even the low-fat version. I often make the same pitas using mashed feta cheese and hot paprika—of course without honey—to serve as appetizers.

3 cups unbleached all-purpose flour

2 teaspoons baking powder

1 cup low-fat plain yogurt

1 1/2 cups mashed ricotta or well-drained cottage cheese

3–6 teaspoons hot paprika or cayenne pepper to taste

2–3 tablespoons chopped fresh mint (optional)

Olive oil to rub the skillet

About 1/2 cup honey, preferably thyme-scented

In the bowl of a food processor or mixer fitted with dough hooks, place the flour and baking powder and pulse to blend. With the motor running pour the yogurt, then about 2/3 cup warm water through the funnel. Add water slowly, just enough to make a soft dough that forms a ball. Process for about 3 minutes and turn out onto a floured working surface. Let rest for about 20 minutes, while you prepare the filling.

Mix the cheese with the paprika or cayenne pepper, adding the mint if you like.

Divide the dough into 8 pieces and form a ball with one each. With a floured rolling pin flatten one—keeping the rest covered with a moist kitchen towel—to obtain a 10-to 12-inch round disk. It doesn't matter if it isn't a perfect circle. Take about 2 tablespoons of the filling and spread it over the dough. Roll up like a cigar, as tightly as you can. Coil the roll, sticking its end in so the filling won't come out. Sprinkle lightly with flour and roll again with the rolling pin to obtain a flat disk about 10 inches in diameter.

Cover and repeat with the rest of the dough.

Warm a heavy 12-inch nonstick skillet and rub a small amount of olive oil over it with a paper towel. Place one pita in the skillet and cook, pressing down with a wooden spatula, for about 3 minutes. Turn over with the spatula and cook on the other side for another 2 to 3 minutes. The cooked pita will have brown speckles. Transfer to a serving dish and drizzle with honey while hot.

Continue cooking the pitas and stack them one on top of the other, pouring honey over each one.

While still warm, cut the whole stack in wedges to serve.

Serves 8.

Honey & Bulgur Pudding

This dessert complements a very spicy meal perfectly. I found it on the Greek island of Kythera. The island produces delicious thyme honey, and its fragrance dominates this simple pudding. People make the pudding in July, boiling their recently harvested stone-ground wheat in honeyed water—the water that was used to clean honeycombs.

Because this dessert consists of just honey, grains, and some spices, I think it must be one of the first ever devised. I came across a similar dessert in Oded Schwartz's book *In Search of Plenty, A History of Jewish Food*. The recipe—in which the bulgur is cooked in milk and honey—was included in the chapter entitled "Biblical and Historic Recipes." You can make this pudding as sweet as you like by increasing the amount of honey.

1 cup bulgur, coarse or medium grain
¾ cup honey (preferably Greek thyme honey), or more to taste
1½ teaspoons dried Mediterranean thyme, tied in a piece of cheesecloth
1 cinnamon stick, about 2 inches long
½ cup dried Zante currants
⅔ cup freshly roasted and coarsely chopped almonds
Ground cinnamon, for sprinkling

Place the bulgur in a large pot and cover with about 2½ quarts water. Bring to a boil and simmer for about 30 minutes. Add the honey, thyme, and cinnamon stick and continue simmering for another 20 minutes, checking often and stirring with a wooden spoon from time to time.

Add the currants and a little more water, if needed, and simmer for another 20 to 30 minutes, until the liquid has thickened. Taste and add more honey if you like.

Remove from the heat, discard the thyme and cinnamon stick, and divide the pudding among 8 bowls. Sprinkle with the roasted almonds and some cinnamon and let cool completely. Place in the refrigerator and chill for 2 to 3 hours, or overnight, before serving.

Serves 8.

VARIATION: Add a teaspoon of ground white pepper to make a hot-sweet pudding.

Spicy Mastic Ice Cream

Mastic-scented ice cream is a delicious, exotic finish to any meal. Mastic (often confused with the tasteless gum arabic, which it resembles), is the fragrant resin from a member of the pistachio family that grows only on the Greek island of Chios. Used from antiquity all over the Middle East as a chewing gum and to flavor sweets, mastic is also an excellent flavoring for breads and cookies. You can get it in specialty stores.

Salep (or sahalep), the powdered root of wild *orchis* species, was traditionally used to thicken the ice cream. This powder, which is also mixed with sugar, cinnamon, and water and served as a beverage, was considered by ancient Greeks to be an aphrodisiac. But it is difficult to find in the United States, so use arrowroot or cornstarch instead.

In my version of this classic Greek ice cream, dried chili is added to the boiling milk, giving it an unexpected hot flavor. Serve by itself, or with fruit salads or fruit tarts.

6 egg yolks

1 cup sugar

2 cups whole milk

1 dried chili, seeded and cut in half lengthwise

2 teaspoons arrowroot or cornstarch

1 teaspoon mastic (see Mail-Order Sources), powdered in a mortar with a little granulated sugar (see Note)

1 cup thick yogurt (see page 103) or cream

Beat the egg yolks with the sugar until they turn light yellow.

In a pot over medium heat, warm the milk with the chili and arrowroot or cornstarch, stirring constantly, until it thickens. Remove the chili and slowly pour the milk over the egg and sugar mixture while whisking at a low speed. Be careful not to let the eggs get too hot so they scramble.

Return the mixture to the pot and, stirring constantly, bring to a boil over low heat. Cook for 1 to 2 minutes, until the cream thickens. Pass through a fine sieve into a bowl, add the mastic and yogurt or cream, and stir vigorously for a few seconds.

Let cool completely, placing the bowl in a larger container filled with ice cubes. Stir from time to time until completely cold.

Place in an ice-cream machine and freeze according to the manufacturer's instructions.

Makes 1 quart.

NOTE: Keep mastic in the freezer. It can be powdered easily in a mortar when frozen. Use a stone or porcelain mortar, because mastic sticks to wood.

Cream Cheese Tart with Dried Fruit & Pine Nuts

I got the idea for a sweet and peppery tart from descriptions of ancient desserts, which combined sweet and spicy tastes freely. Apicius—who wrote the first surviving cookbook, in Roman times—lists a dessert made with cream cheese and dried fruits that reminded me of the Cardinal d'Este's tart in Lynne Rossetto-Kasper's marvelous book about the cooking of Emilia-Romagna, *The Splendid Table*. She writes that the tart is "edible time travel from the 16th century," but I think it goes much further back in history. My tart is based on her recipe.

PASTRY

1 cup all-purpose flour
Pinch of ground cinnamon
3 tablespoons light olive oil
Tiny pinch of saffron

Tiny pinch of salt
3 tablespoons confectioners' sugar
1 egg, lightly beaten
1 ½ cups ricotta or cream cheese

FILLING

½ –⅔ cup granulated sugar, plus
    1 tablespoon for top
2 eggs
1 tablespoon grated orange zest
6–8 grindings of black pepper, plus
    additional for top
1 teaspoon ground cinnamon, plus
    additional for top

½ cup raisins and ½ cup chopped
    dried apricots, soaked in fortified sweet
    wine, such as Pineau de Charente,
    Samos Vin de Liqueur, or Vernaccia
    from Sardinia
3–4 tablespoons toasted pine nuts

Place the flour, cinnamon, olive oil, saffron, salt, and confectioners' sugar in the bowl of a food processor. Process very briefly until you have a mixture that resembles large bread crumbs. Add the egg and pulse briefly, just until the pastry holds together. Form a ball with the pastry and flatten it into a disk. With your fingers, press the dough into a 10-inch tart pan, lining the bottom and sides with an equally thick layer. Cover with plastic wrap and let stand in the refrigerator for at least 1 hour or overnight.

Preheat the oven to 375°F.

Prick the bottom of the pastry shell with the tines of a fork. Cover the shell, including the rim, with aluminum foil, pressing down so the crust keeps its form during baking. Fill the foil with rice, beans, or baking weights and bake for 10 to 15 minutes; let stand for 5 minutes on a rack before removing the foil. Bake for another 10 to 15 minutes, until crust just starts to turn golden. Let cool completely. Readjust the oven to 350°F.

Beat the ricotta with the sugar, eggs, orange zest, pepper, and cinnamon until creamy. Drain the dried fruits and add them to the cheese mixture and stir to blend. Spread the mixture evenly over the cooled tart shell and bake for about 20 minutes, until the filling starts to set. Sprinkle with the sugar, some more pepper, and more cinnamon. Arrange the pine nuts on top and continue baking for another 15 to 20 minutes, until a toothpick inserted in the center of the filling comes out clean.

Let cool completely on a rack before serving.
Serves 6 to 8.

Caramelized Stuffed Figs in Almond Liqueur

At a dinner my friend, Israeli food writer Dalia Lamdani, gave for me in her home in Tel Aviv, she served delicious almond-stuffed figs in heavy syrup. Trying to lighten up Dalia's recipe, I came up with the following spirited version. Serve with thick yogurt, heavy cream, or vanilla ice cream.

1 ½ cups sweet wine such as Pineau de Charente, Samos Vin de Liqueur, or Vernaccia from Sardinia

1 pound dried figs (about 16 figs), preferably from Greece, Turkey, or another Mediterranean country

⅓ cup blanched almonds

⅓ cup almond liqueur, mixed with a pinch of freshly ground pepper, ground cinnamon, cloves, and nutmeg

3 tablespoons light brown sugar

Thick yogurt (see page 103), cream, or vanilla ice cream (optional)

In a medium nonreactive pan warm the wine and 1 cup water, then add the figs. Bring to a boil, lower the heat, and simmer for 20 to 30 minutes or until tender. Remove with a slotted spoon and let cool a little. Stuff the bottom end of each fig with 2 or 3 almonds and place in a serving dish that just holds the figs in one layer.

Mix the cooking liquid with the liqueur and pour over the figs. Sprinkle with the brown sugar and place under the broiler for a few minutes to caramelize. Spoon tablespoons of the sauce over the figs, cover with aluminum foil, and let cool for 4 to 5 hours, or overnight, before serving.

Serve with thick yogurt, cream, or vanilla ice cream.

Serves 4.

Appendix

Buying & Using Spices & Chilies

The majority of spices still come to us from the East, but they are no longer precious, as they were in the Middle Ages. India is the leading exporter of most spices, but other Asian countries—such as Indonesia, Madagascar, and Malaysia—also produce pepper, cardamom, ginger, cinnamon and cassia, cloves, and vanilla. The fragile economies of many Third World countries depend heavily on their spice exports. Millions of families work in labor-intensive spice plantations, cultivating the plants and picking and drying the fragrant products that find their way to our markets.

Picking spices from supermarket shelves is easy and convenient, but not the best way to get the finest products. In many North American cities there are Middle Eastern and Asian markets selling—among other things—a variety of spices. Those are the best places to look for fresher and more fragrant products. There are also excellent mail-order sources (page 104) if you are trying to locate unusual spices.

When buying spices looks can often be deceiving. Trust your sense of smell and taste. To achieve the most flavorful results, buy whole spices and grind small quantities—enough to last a couple of weeks—in a clean coffee mill or spice grinder, or pound them in a mortar. If you find exceptionally good spices, buy larger quantities and freeze in airtight containers.

Cooking with spices requires practice, imagination, and a well-stocked spice shelf. The amounts suggested in the recipes are just starting points. The taste, pungency, and aroma of each spice or spice mixture varies according to the country of origin, the year of production, the freshness, the method of drying, and so forth.

In regional North African and Middle Eastern cookbooks, the amount of peppercorns, chilies, and other spices is hardly ever specified. Cooks there don't measure. Working from experience, they add a pinch of this or that. Most families have their own special spice combinations, which are often a closely guarded secret, transmitted only to the following generation.

To learn the fine art of spicing, one can only rely on trial and error. Start with small amounts, taste, and add more. Bear in mind that freshly cooked stews, for example, need to mellow for a few hours or overnight before the final flavor of the dish develops. Taste the stew again the next day to adjust the seasoning.

Freezing foods that contain chilies increases the pungency of the dish, because the flesh of the capsicums breaks, releasing more heat.

Always buy whole peppercorns. Black peppercorns are produced by drying unripe berries after leaving them to ferment for a few days. Black pepper is fragrant and hot, and should be ground just before using. Several varieties—such as the strong and pungent Tellicherry and the more subtle Malabar—are available at good spice shops. As a general rule, ask for the best quality—uniform hard peppercorns without twigs. Whole peppercorns will keep for years, so it is worth buying in quantity. White peppercorns are dried ripe peppercorns with the skins removed. White pepper is more pungent, less fragrant, and more expensive. I use it to flavor white sauces, soft cheeses, and sweets, because I prefer the more complex taste of black pepper for most dishes. But it is clearly a matter of taste; try the same dish with black and white pepper, to see which you prefer. Green peppercorns, which are less hot, are unripe berries preserved in brine or freeze-dried. Pink peppercorns (Schinus molle) are not related to pepper. The easily crushed pink peppercorns are not hot but fragrant, with a sour aftertaste. They are used for their aroma, mainly in dressings and sauces.

Although we call them peppers, the only thing chilies have in common with the peppercorns is heat. They belong to the family of solanaceae—which also includes potatoes, tomatoes, and tobacco—and were introduced to Europe from the New World by Christopher Columbus. Capsicum annum is the botanical name for most of the hot and milder chilies that are grown today all over the world. They vary greatly in heat—not only between different kinds, but often within the same batch—from mild to blisteringly hot. Even if two chilies look alike, their taste and pungency may be very different, depending on the soil and climate of their places of origin. Jalapeños and fresh red and green chilies can be used in the recipes of this book; they

are the most readily available substitutes for the various capsicums grown around the Mediterranean. You may also want to add some poblanos to the more pungent but less flavorful jalapeños or other chilies for taste. Most peppers around the Mediterranean are left to ripen on the vine, which gives them a deeper flavor. One can easily grow chilies in a pot on a sunny balcony or window sill, if you live in a warm climate with plenty of sun.

If you want a more authentic Mediterranean taste, use Aleppo or Near East pepper, usually imported from Turkey or Syria. Moderately hot red chilies—ripened on the vine—are sun-dried, seeded, and crushed. Supermarket red pepper flakes are no substitute for Aleppo pepper. They are much hotter, without any other distinguishable flavor. Turkish pepper paste is delicious, with a deep flavor; it can be used in sauces and stews. Good Hungarian paprika—a combination of mild paprika with a little hot mixed in—is also used in the Mediterranean, especially in the Balkans and in Israel. The delicious pimenton picante of Spain is not easy to find in North America, while the often extremely hot Italian peperoncini are only rarely found in Italian markets. But this shouldn't be a problem. A tremendous variety of hot peppers—both fresh and dried—are available all over North America. I suggest that you experiment, substituting different combinations of hotter and milder American capsicums—for example New Mexican chilies with poblanos or anchos—for the chilies suggested in the recipes of this book. Small amounts of chipotle chilies (smoked jalapeños) will add another dimension to most Mediterranean dishes, especially stews.

RAS EL HANOUT

This is probably the most mysterious and enchanting of all spice mixtures. It comes from Morocco, and its name means the "top of the shop." In its classic form it contains no less than twenty-seven different spices, aromatics, and aphrodisiacs, including Spanish fly (*cantharis*) and grains of paradise (see introduction).

I had the privilege to go to a marvelous old spice shop in Marrakech with Paula Wolfert, *the* expert on Moroccan cooking. With her well-researched list of ingredients at hand, we watched the merchant's assistant assemble the blend. But Paula made me swear that I would never grind this marvelously colorful *ras el hanout*. "It might be dangerous for your health," she said. So I keep my unground mixture in a jar and inhale its wonderful aroma from time to time. For cooking, I use a simpler mixture, which is still delicious. You will also find *ras el hanout* mixtures in good specialty stores via direct mail (see Mail-Order Sources).

The following recipe is Paula Wolfert's, from her classic book *Couscous and Other Good Food from Morocco*.

Use *Ras el Hanout* to flavor game, lamb, meat stews, couscous, and meat and chicken soups.

1 teaspoon cumin seeds
1 teaspoon ground ginger
1 ½ teaspoons coriander seeds
1 ½ teaspoons black peppercorns
¼ teaspoon cayenne pepper
4 whole cloves

6 allspice berries
1 ½ teaspoons ground cinnamon

Grind all the spices in a clean coffee mill or spice grinder. Store in an airtight jar.
Makes about 2 ½ tablespoons.

GRATED TOMATOES

Instead of blanching and peeling tomatoes, in Greece we simply grate them. Halve the tomato and cut out the hard stem. Holding it with the cut side facing a coarse grater, grate over a bowl. You will end up with just the skin, which you can discard. If you want to remove the seeds— something that is not usually done in Greece and the Middle East—lightly squeeze the halved tomato before grating it. But the liquid around the seeds is very flavorful. Use grated tomatoes whenever tomato pulp is called for in a recipe.

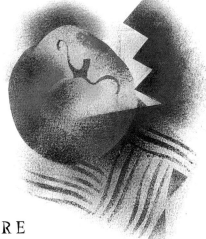

ETHIOPIAN BERBERE

In a small shop near the old bus station in Tel Aviv that sells Ethiopian baskets, lovely handwoven fabrics, and a few spices, my friend Dalia Lamdani—an Israeli food editor— tried to decipher for me the secrets of this basic Ethiopian spice mixture. In the tiny Ethiopian restaurant across the street, Eden Dassa, the owner, told us that the mixture was called *mitmita* and contained twelve ingredients, one of which, in translation, means "man's health." We couldn't find all the ingredients for the mixture in the shop, but we learned the basic formula for the spice mixture, which is better known as Ethiopian *berbere*. (*Berbere* means "hot pepper" in one of the Ethiopian dialects.)

Korerima, the cardamom in the Ethiopian shop, is a wild variety that looks like small dried figs and has a stronger flavor than green or white cardamom.

Ethiopian *berbere* is delicious, and is mainly used to flavor the meat stew that accompanies the gruel that constitutes the common Ethiopian meal. Nevertheless, you can use it to season any meat stew or soup.

1 teaspoon ground ginger
3–4 teaspoons red pepper flakes
1 teaspoon black peppercorns
Seeds from 8–10 white cardamom pods
½ teaspoon fenugreek
½ teaspoon nigella seeds (optional; see Mail-Order Sources)
3–5 whole cloves
6 allspice berries

1 piece cinnamon stick, 2 to 3 inches long
1 small pinch ajwain seeds (see Mail-Order Sources) or caraway seeds

Grind all the spices in a clean coffee mill or spice grinder to a fine powder. Store in an airtight jar.
    Makes about 4 tablespoons.

TABIL

Tabil, the basic Tunisian spice mixture, always contains garlic. Although it seems unusual to include garlic in a spice mixture, throughout the Middle East and North Africa, most of the garlic used is in the form of dehydrated garlic flakes. They are frequently soaked in water to be reconstituted, then pickled and served as an appetizer. Be sure to use dried minced garlic. Substituting garlic powder isn't a good idea.

As with all spice mixtures there are many variations of *tabil*. Here is a simple version based loosely on the recipe given in Mohamed Koulki's book *Cuisine et Patisserie Tunisienne*. Use Tabil to flavor stewed meat or poultry, couscous, and soups.

1 tablespoon red pepper flakes
1 tablespoon coriander seeds
1 tablespoon caraway seeds
1 teaspoon dehydrated garlic flakes

Grind spices in a clean coffee mill or spice grinder and store in an airtight jar.
    Makes about 3 tablespoons.

MEDITERRANEAN RED PEPPER PASTE

I got the idea for this delicious condiment from Ayla Algar's *Classical Turkish Cooking*. According to her, in the summer the rooftops of the village houses in southeastern Turkey are covered with bright red pepper paste that has been left to dry in the sun.

Because the ordinary red bell peppers from supermarkets have very little flavor, I suggest you mix them with roasted Spanish or Greek red peppers sold in jars or use some pimientos with the chilies or jalapeños. Before using the fresh jalapeños, hang them in an airy place for a few days until they turn red. Instead of simmering the peppers in water, as is the custom in Turkey, I sauté mine in olive oil and then cook them in red wine, which gives the resulting paste a deeper flavor.

Use Red Pepper Paste instead of tomato paste, or mix the two, to season stews and soups.

Mix with fruity extra-virgin olive oil and serve in small bowls with fresh bread for dipping or brush on pita or stale bread slices and broil them to serve as a snack or to accompany soups and spreads.

Add to salad dressings, especially vinaigrettes for steamed vegetables or grilled or steamed fish.

To make a hot pink mayonnaise, add 1 to 2 teaspoons Red Pepper Paste to a cup of mayonnaise.

2 pounds red bell peppers or a mixture of bell
   peppers and pimientos mixed with well-
   drained Spanish or Greek red peppers
   sold in jars
½ pound fresh red chili peppers (or red
   jalapeños)
½ cup olive oil, plus more for topping the jars
1 cup dry red wine
1 ½ teaspoons coarse sea salt

Wash, dry, and seed all the peppers. Cut them into ½-inch slices. In a nonreactive large sauté pan or deep skillet, warm the olive oil and sauté the peppers for 10 to 15 minutes, stirring often, until soft. Pour in the wine, cover with a piece of parch-ment paper or aluminum foil, and let the peppers simmer for about 20 minutes. Add the salt and ½ cup water and continue simmering covered for another 25 to 30 minutes, until very soft and mushy.

Pass the mixture through a food mill and place in a pan in which the paste does not come higher than ½ inch. Let the paste dry in a very low (170°F.) oven for 5 ½ to 6 hours, until very thick. Alter-nately, you can dry it in batches in a microwave. Let cool, transfer to jars, top with olive oil, and store in the refrigerator.

Red Pepper Paste keeps for about 2 months and can be frozen.

Makes about 2 cups.

HARISSA (TUNISIAN HOT CHILI PASTE)

Harissa is one of the most delicious hot condiments I have tasted. Although you will find it readily available in specialty stores, it is worth the small effort to make your own, because it tastes so much better.

A version of this recipe was included in my previous book, *The Mediterranean Pantry*, and is loosely based on Paula Wolfert's recipe as it appeared in her classic book *Mediter-ranean Cooking*. Paula introduced me to *harissa* before I had the opportunity to taste it in Tunisia.

I prefer to use Aleppo pepper, because the dense flavor of that extraordinary pepper makes the *Harissa* even better, although it is not exactly what cooks in North Africa would normally do.

Use Harissa to flavor stews, especially the ones containing tomatoes. Harissa is also excellent in salad dressings for raw or steamed vegetables.

5–6 tablespoons extra-virgin olive oil, or more as needed

4 teaspoons minced garlic

⅓ cup Aleppo pepper (see Mail-Order Sources) or dried New Mexican chilies

½ teaspoon ground coriander

2 teaspoons ground caraway seeds

Warm 2 tablespoons of olive oil in a small skillet and sauté the garlic until soft, without letting it color, about 1 minute.

In a food processor work the pepper with the coriander, caraway, and sautéed garlic, adding 2 teaspoons of water and 1 to 2 tablespoons olive oil to make a thick paste (more water and olive oil may be needed).

Pack tightly in a small jar and top with some olive oil to cover. Keep in the refrigerator. Harissa keeps for 3 months or more.

Makes a little more than ⅓ cup.

NOTE: If you are using New Mexican chilies, remove the stems and seeds and soak in warm water for 10 to 20 minutes. Wrap in cheesecloth and press well to remove as much liquid as possible, then proceed as described above. In this case, no additional water is needed.

PICKLED CHILI PEPPER PASTE

Hot and sour, this very different pungent pepper paste can be used instead of fresh chilies or jalapeños in salad dressings and spreads.

½ pound long green chilies or jalapeños

2–3 tablespoons coriander seeds

5 large garlic cloves, halved lengthwise

2 bay leaves

1 cup cider vinegar

About 2 cups distilled white vinegar

Wash and dry the chilies. Slash each one with a knife, so that the vinegar will penetrate them quickly. Pack them very tightly in a 1-quart jar, sprinkle with the coriander, add the garlic and bay leaves, and add the vinegars to cover the chilies completely. Let macerate for at least 4 weeks at room temperature, shaking occasionally.

Remove the peppers, cut off the stems, discard the seeds, and place them in a blender or food processor. Process to obtain a smooth paste, adding 1 tablespoon of the liquid from the jar to facilitate the process if needed. Place the paste in a jar, cover tightly, and store in the refrigerator. It will keep for more than a year.

Makes about 1 1/2 cups.

NOTE: Reserve the pungent vinegar in which the chilies have macerated and use small amounts in salad dressings. It is very good in mayonnaise.

CHILI OLIVE OIL

I always keep a bottle of this hot olive oil in my pantry. I love to mix a few teaspoons into salad dressings. I also love it on all kinds of breads and focaccias. But it has many more uses. Brush commercial pita bread (I prefer whole wheat) with some Chili Olive Oil, and broil for a couple of minutes on each side. Serve with grilled vegetables, dips, or cheese. Brush zucchini or eggplant slices with the oil, sprinkle with salt, and broil or grill over charcoal. Add a little oil to salad dressings, especially for broccoli and potatoes but also for fresh tomato or mixed salads. Brush fish, meat, or poultry fillets with Chili Olive Oil on both sides. Let stand for 30 minutes before broiling or grilling.

You can make it hotter or milder by varying the amount of chilies.

1 cup plus 1 tablespoon fruity extra-virgin olive oil

4–6 teaspoons Aleppo pepper (see Mail-Order Sources), or 3–5 small dried chilies, cut into small pieces with a pair of scissors

In a small skillet, warm 2 tablespoons of the olive oil and add the pepper. Stir a few times with a wooden spoon and remove from the heat as the pepper releases its fragrance, about 2 minutes. Be careful not to let it burn.

Let it cool. Transfer to a jar or bottle, top with the rest of the olive oil, and shake to mix. Store in a dark, cool place for about 1 week. Pass through a fine sieve and store in a dark place. Chili Olive Oil will keep for about 6 months.

Makes 1 cup.

VARIATION: You can add 1 tablespoon of dried Mediterranean oregano, rosemary, or sage—or any herb you like—as you take the skillet off the heat. Proceed as described above to make different flavors of Chili Olive Oil.

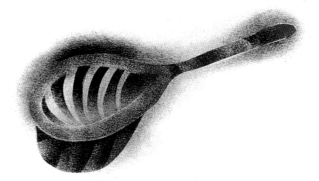

DRAINING YOGURT

Thick yogurt like that which is available in Greece and the Middle East is difficult to find in North America, but you can easily drain regular or low-fat yogurt so it reaches the required consistency. Drained yogurt is frequently called yogurt cheese.

Line a sieve or colander with double cheesecloth, add a little salt to the yogurt, stir, and pour into the cheesecloth. Place the sieve over a bowl to collect the whey, which you can use instead of water for cooking vegetables or add to soups.

Depending on the consistency of the yogurt you are draining, you should bear in mind that the yogurt will lose about ¼ of its volume after an hour's draining. That means that if you need 1 cup thick yogurt, you should drain 1¼ cups.

After one hour, the yogurt will have the right consistency for sauces. If you want it thicker, leave it to drain longer. Needless to say, its volume will be further reduced.

Lightly salted, drained yogurt keeps well in a covered container in the refrigerator for more than 2 weeks, so you can make more than you need each time.

Mail-Order Sources

Adriana's Caravan
409 Vanderbilt Street
Brooklyn, N.Y.
(mail-order only;
catalogue available)
718-436-8565
800-316-0820

Near East or Aleppo pepper,
mastic, nigella, fenugreek, chilis,
extra virgin olive oil, bulgur,
couscous.

Dean and DeLuca
560 Broadway
New York, NY 10012
212-431-1691
800-221-7714

Near East or Aleppo pepper.

Hollow Road Farms
R.R. 1, Box 93
Stuyvesant, NY 12173
518-758-7214

Write for names of nearest sup-
pliers of sheep's milk yogurt.

Kalustyan
123 Lexington Avenue
New York, NY 10016
(catalogue available)
212-685-3451

Near East or Aleppo and Turkish
pepper, Turkish pepper paste,
nigella, capers preserved in salt.

Oriental Pastry and Grocery
170-172 Atlantic Avenue
Brooklyn, NY 11201
718-875-7687

Near East or Aleppo pepper,
mastic, mahlep.

Paprikas Weiss Importer
1572 Second Avenue
New York, NY 10028
(catalogue available)
212-288-6117
fax 212-734-5120

Mastic, chili peppers, fenugreek,
bread flour, couscous.

Penzeys, Ltd.
P.O. Box 1448
Waukesha, WI 53187
414-574-0277
fax 414-574-0278

Fenugreek, black, white, and
pink peppercorns.

Shallah's Middle Eastern
Importing Company
290 White Street
Danbury, CT 06810
203-743-4181

Near East or Aleppo pepper,
mahlep, mastic, nigella.

Sultan's Delight
P.O. Box 090302
Brooklyn, NY 11209
(mail-order only; catalogue
available)
718-745-6844
800-852-5046
fax 718-745-2563

Mahlep, mastic, nigella,
falafel molds, olive oils, bulgur,
couscous, and olives.

Zingerman's Deli
422 Detroit Street
Ann Arbor, MI 48104
313-769-1625

Spanish hot and sweet paprika
(pimenton), Turkish pepper flakes
and pepper paste, Aleppo pepper.

Conversions

WEIGHT EQUIVALENTS

The metric weights given in this chart are not exact equivalents, but have been rounded up or down slightly to make measuring easier.

Avoirdupois	Metric
¼ oz	7 g
½ oz	15 g
1 oz	30 g
2 oz	60 g
3 oz	90 g
4 oz	115 g
5 oz	150 g
6 oz	175 g
7 oz	200 g
8 oz (½ lb)	225 g
9 oz	250 g
10 oz	300 g
11 oz	325 g
12 oz	350 g
13 oz	375 g
14 oz	400 g
15 oz	425 g
16 oz (1 lb)	450 g
1 lb 2 oz	500 g
1½ lb	750 g
2 lb	900 g
2¼ lb	1 kg
3 lb	1.4 kg
4 lb	1.8 kg
4½ lb	2 kg

VOLUME EQUIVALENTS

These are not exact equivalents for the American cups and spoons, but have been rounded up or down slightly to make measuring easier.

American	Metric	Imperial
¼ t	1.25 ml	
½ t	2.5 ml	
1 t	5 ml	
½ T (1½ t)	7.5 ml	
1 T (3 t)	15 ml	
¼ cup (4 T)	60 ml	2 fl. oz
⅓ cup (5 T)	75 ml	2½ fl oz
½ cup (8 T)	125 ml	4 fl oz
⅔ cup (10 T)	150 ml	5 fl oz (¼ pint)
¾ cup (12 T)	175 ml	6 fl oz (⅓ pint)
1 cup (16 T)	250 ml	8 fl oz
1¼ cups	300 ml	10 fl oz (½ pint)
1½ cups	350 ml	12 fl oz
1 pint (2 cups)	500 ml	16 fl oz
2½ cups	575 ml	20 fl oz (1 pint)
1 quart (4 cups)	1 litre	1¾ pints

OVEN TEMPERATURE EQUIVALENTS

Oven	°F.	°C.	Gas Mark
very cool	250–275	130–140	½–1
cool	300	150	2
warm	325	170	3
moderate	350	180	4
moderately hot	375	190	5
	400	200	6
hot	425	220	7
very hot	450	230	8
	475	250	9

Bibliography

Algar, Ayla. *Classical Turkish Cooking*. New York: Harper Collins, 1991.

Andrews, Jean. *Red Hot Peppers*. New York: Macmillan, 1993.

_____. *Peppers, The Domesticated Capsicums*. Austin: University of Texas Press, 1984.

Antreassian, Alice. *Armenian Cooking Today*. New York: St. Vartan Press, 1989.

Athenaeus. *The Deipnosophists*. Loeb Classical Library. Cambridge, Mass.: Harvard University Press, 1971.

Baysal, Ayse. *Samples from Turkish Cuisine*. Ankara: Turkish Historical Society, 1993.

Benghiat, Suzy. *Middle Eastern Cooking*. New Jersey: Chartwell Books, Inc., 1984.

Blanc, Nicole and Anne Nercessian. *La cuisine Romaine Antique*. Paris: Glenat, Faton, 1982.

Bolens, Lucie. *La cuisine Andalouse, un Art de Vivre XI-XII siecle*. Paris: Albin Michel, 1990.

Bouayed, Fatima-Zohra. *La Cuisine Algerienne*. Paris: Temps Actuel, 1983.

Bugialli, Giuliano. *The Fine Art of Italian Cooking*. New York: Times Books, 1977.

Coe, Sophie. *America's First Cuisines*. Austin: University of Texas Books, 1994.

David, Elizabeth. *A Book of Mediterranean Food*. London: Penguin, 1965.

_____. *Summer Cooking*. London: Dorling Kindersley, 1988.

_____. "Mad, mad, despised and dangerous." Petits Propos Culinaires 9. London: Prospect Books, 1981.

Davidson, Alan. *Mediterranean Seafood*. London: Penguin Books, 1981.

Dinia, Hayat. *La Cuisine Marocaine de Rabat*. Rabat: Ribat el Fath, 1990.

Dougall, Anton. *A Taste of Malta*. Valetta: Klabb Tat-Tisjir, 1993.

Edwards, John. *The Roman Cookery of Apicius*. Washington, D.C.: Hartley and Marks, 1984.

Eren, Neset. *The Delights of Turkish Cooking*. Istanbul: Redhouse Yavinevi, 1988.

Field, Carol. *Celebrating Italy*. New York: William Morrow, 1990.

_____. *The Italian Baker*. New York: Harper and Row, 1985.

_____. *Italy in Small Bites*. New York: William Morrow, 1993.

Gedda, Guy. *La Table d'un Provencal*. Paris: Roland Escaing, 1989.

Ganor, Avi and Maiberg, Ron. *A Taste of Israel*. New York: Rizzoli, 1990.

Gozzini, Giacosa Ilaria. *A Taste of Ancient Rome*. Chicago: University of Chicago Press, 1992.

Gray, Patience. *Honey from a Weed*. San Francisco: North Point Press, 1990.

Hadjiat, Salima. *La Cuisine d'Algerie*. Paris: Publisud, 1990.

Halici, Nevin. *Turkish Cookbook*. London: Dorling Kindersley, 1989.

Haroutunian, Arto der. *A Turkish Cookbook*. London: Ebury Press, 1987.

_____. *Yogurt Book*. London: Penguin Books, 1984.

Hazan, Marcella. *The Essentials of Classic Italian Cooking*. London: Macmillan, 1992.

Helou, Anissa. *Lebanese Cuisine*. London: Grub Street, 1994.

Henisch, Bridget Ann. *Feast and Fast*. London: University Park, 1994.

Huygue, Edith et Francois-Bernard. *Les coureures d'Epices*. Paris: J. Clattes, 1994.

Karaoglan, Aida. *Food for the Vegetarian: Traditional Lebanese Recipes*. New York: Interlink Books, 1988.

Kasper, Lynne Rossetto. *The Splendid Table*. New York: William Morrow, 1992.

Kouki, Mohamed. *Cuisine et Patisserie Tunisiennes*. Tunis, 1987.

Lassalle, George. *East of Orphanides*. London: Kyle Cathie, Ltd., 1991.

Levy-Mellul, Rivka. *La Cuisine Juive Marocaine*. Mont-Royal, Quebec: Phidal, 1994.

Liddell and Scott. *Greek-English Lexicon*. Oxford: Oxford University Press, 1969.

Lissen, A. and S. Cleary. *Tapas*. London: Apple Press, 1989.

Luard, Elisabeth. *Tapas*. Cambridge: Martin Books, 1991.

Mallos, Tess. *The Complete Middle East Cookbook*. London: Peter Ward, 1990.

McGee, Harold. *The Curious Cook*. New York: Collier-Macmillan, 1992.

_____. *On Food and Cooking*. London: Harper Collins, 1991.

Mesfin, Daniel. *Exotic Ethiopian Cooking*. Falls Church, Va.: Ethiopian Cookbook Enterprises, 1993.

Mourtzis, Marios. *The Cooking In Cyprus*. (In Greek). Nicosia: Morfotiki, n.d.

Naj, Amal. *Peppers, A Story of Hot Pursuits*. New York: Vintage Books, 1993.

Nathan, Joan. *Jewish Cooking in America*. New York: Alfred Knopf, 1994.

Navarro, Evelyne et Ambroise. *Manuel des Gourmandises Pied-Noir*. Bayonne: Jean Curutchet, Editions Harriet, 1993.

Norman, Jill. *The Complete Book of Spices*. London: Dorling Kindersley, 1990.

Piceci, Tonio. *Oltre le Orecchiette*. Lecce: Edizioni del Grifo, 1994.

Ramazanoglu, Gulseren. *Turkish Cooking*. Istanbul: Ramazanoglu Publications, 1992.

Rayess, George. *The Art of Lebanese Cooking*. Beirut: Librarie du Liban, 1982.

Rinzler, Carol Ann. *Herbs, Spices, and Condiments*. New York: Henry Holt & Co., 1990.

Roden, Claudia. *The Food of Italy*. London: Arrow Books, 1990.

_____. *Mediterranean Cookery*. London: BBC Books, 1992.

_____. *A New Book of Middle Eastern Food*. London: Penguin, 1963.

Saberi, Helen. *Afghan Food and Cookery*. London: Prospect Books, 1986.

Schivelbusch, Wolfgang. *Tastes of Paradise*. New York: Pantheon Books, 1992.

Schneider, Elizabeth. *Uncommon Fruits and Vegetables: A Commonsense Guide*. New York: Harper Perennial, 1990.

Schwarz, Oded. *In Search of Plenty, A History of Jewish Food*. London: Kyle Cathie Ltd., 1992.

Servi Machlin, Edda. *The Classic Cuisine of the Italian Jews*. New York: Everest House, 1981.

Sevilla, Maria Jose. *Spain on a Plate*. London: BBC Books, 1992.

Shaida, Margaret. *The Legendary Cuisine of Persia*. London: Penguin, 1994.

Shihab, Aziz. *A Taste of Palestine, Menus and Memories*. San Antonio: Corona Publishing Co., 1993.

Simeti, Mary Taylor. *On Peresphone's Island*. San Francisco: North Point Press, 1986.

_____. *Pomp and Sustenance*. New York: Henry Holt & Co., 1991.

Spicing Up the Palate: Proceedings of the Oxford Symposium on Food and Cookery 1992. London: Prospect Books, 1992.

Stavroulakis, Nicholas. *Cookbook of the Jews of Greece*. New York: Cadmus Press, 1986.

Stobart, Tom. *Herbs, Spices, and Flavorings*. Woodstock, New York: The Overlook Press, 1970.

Tamzali, Haydee. *La cuisine en Afrique du Nord*. Tunis: Michael Tomkinson, 1990.

Thesaurus Linguae Graecae (CD ROM). Irvine: University of California, 1987.

Toussaint-Samat, Maguelonne. *History of Food*. Cambridge, MA: Blackwell, 1993.

Vergé, Roger. *Vegetables in the French Style*. New York: Artisan, 1994.

Waines, David. *In a Caliph's Kitchen*. London: Rad el Rayyes Books, 1989.

Wirth, Caroline. *Le Meilleur de la Cuisine Maltaise*. Narni-Terni: Plurigraf, 1994.

Wolfert, Paula. *The Cooking of the Eastern Mediterranean*. New York: Harper Collins, 1994.

_____. *Couscous and Other Good Food from Morocco*. New York: Harper Perennial, 1989.

_____. *Mediterranean Cooking*. New York: Ecco Press, 1985.

_____. *Paula Wolfert's World of Food*. New York: Harper and Row, 1988.

Wolf-Cohen, Elisabeth. *New Jewish Cooking*. London: Apple Press, 1993.

Index

DESIGNED BY JIM WAGEMAN,
JENNIFER S. HONG, AND RUSSELL HASSELL

TYPEFACES IN THIS BOOK ARE
GOUDY OLD STYLE, DESIGNED BY FREDERIC W. GOUDY,
AND LA BAMBA, DESIGNED BY DAVID QUAY

PRINTED BY GRAFICHE MILANI,
MILAN, ITALY